OCR7

FROM ADS
TO RICHES

FROM ADS TO RICHES

How to Write
Dynamite Real Estate Classifieds
and Harvest the Results

JOAN McLELLAN TAYLER

Mansion Press
San Francisco, California

Cover design: Sharon Smith
Text design and typesetting: Diane Spencer Hume
Editing: Diane Spencer Hume, David Sweet
Production coordination: Zipporah W. Collins
Printing and binding: Data Reproductions Corporation

Manufactured in the United States of America

Library of Congress Catalog Card number: 94–75764

5 4 3 2 1

To my mother,
artist Vivian Goddard,
on the advent of
her ninetieth birthday

Contents

Foreword

From Ads to Riches is a book clearly written from the vantage point of an expert in the field. Joan Tayler has managed to capture that expertise in a lively and illustrative fashion, covering all the bases and more in the area of writing classified real estate ads.

For those who work in real estate, this will no doubt become an indispensable handbook. Its detail and conversational tone provide insight and digestible information even to those—like me—having no familiarity at all with the subject of writing real estate advertising copy…and that's no easy feat.

Robert H. Waterman, Jr.
Coauthor of *In Search of Excellence*

Preface

"So you're going to write a complete book on classified real estate advertising. Good," said my friends in the real estate business. "I need it. You write it. I'll buy it."

"So you're going to write a book on classified real estate advertising. Hmm…," said my "civilian" friends, no comment…But eventually each one of those noncommittal civilian friends did have something to say about what should be included in the book. It seems they all read classified.

I needed no further encouragement.

From Ads to Riches is a book dedicated to the financial advancement of my fellow residential real estate professionals.

Acknowledgments

My sincere thanks:

To the *San Francisco Chronicle, San Francisco Examiner, San Mateo Times,* and *Boutique and Villager* for putting up with my perfectionism for twenty-five years.

To the memory of that awesome real estate broker Betsy White who proofed my weekly ads.

To Jay, Wendy, Rod, and Garratt, who often said, bless them, "Hey, Mom, this one's a winner!"

To all the good folks who read the Tayler ads and were moved to act upon them.

To the "troops" at JM Tayler & Company Realtors who contributed mightily to the Tayler systems-for-success.

To the author's "resource centers": Max Branscomb, Leigh Robinson, Patti Breitman, Laurie Harper, Vera Cianciolo, Jim Fredrickson, Patrick McGovern, Jr., Mark Dennis, Jean Gwinner, Ken Millichap, Roy Brooks Estate Agents, Women's National Book Association, Burlingame Public Library, and Senior Net.

To author Charlotte E. Thompson, M.D., who got me going and kept me going until this book was done.

What's So Great about Classified Advertising?

sk the ancient Egyptians, who wrote want ads on papyri. Ask the Germans, who were the first to produce want ads on newsprint in 1591. Ask the British, who peddled homes in their newspapers in the 1600s. Ask good old Ben Franklin, who introduced the classified concept to Americans in the *Pennsylvania Gazette* in 1791. These ghosts of classified past will tell you that classified advertising has been "The People's Marketplace" for thirty centuries.

It Is Imprinted in Our Genes

Today there is hardly a literate American over the age of eighteen who has not been touched by classified newspaper advertising, whether to sell a bike, buy a crib, or hunt for a home. Sixty-six percent of the readers of newspapers look at classified. That's **fifty million people!**

The newspaper industry makes over 7 percent of its annual revenues from classified real estate advertising alone. The real estate industry spends over 12 percent of its annual overhead on classified newspaper advertising. According to *Inside the Real Estate Business,* published by the National Association of Realtors, 24 percent of home buyers use newspaper advertising as their primary source of information leading to home purchase. According to the *1990 Scarborough Report,* 61 percent of the potential buyers surveyed in San Mateo County (adjacent to San Francisco County) used daily newspaper classified as their main source of information when shopping for real estate. The fact of the matter is that the public expects residential real estate to be advertised in newspaper classified. Every real estate licensee who sells residential property is in some way involved in the classified process.

Going It Alone

Each month the real estate industry places millions of ads in the classified sections of newspapers. Each month thousands of individuals advertise property for sale and for rent in classified. They do an admirable job of it, considering that no professional education is offered to them on the subject of classified copywriting. (Newspapers train their own staffs, and they put on a smattering of seminars on classified for the benefit of real estate professionals.) Out of the 1,700 books in print on the subject of real estate, would you believe, only a half dozen are available on classified real estate advertising? Apart from what individual brokers might possibly teach in their own offices, those who write classified real estate advertising do so without any schooling.

From Ads to Riches, the only complete book on the classified process, is intended to fill the education gap.

The Job Gets Done

The real estate classified job gets done, without education and guidebooks, because it is a relatively easy job to do, thanks to the accommodation of the newspapers. Anyone with a piece of real estate to sell can call up a newspaper, give a few facts, and know that his ad will be in the hands of 100,000 readers in less than twenty-four hours, for a cost of $25 or less.

Classified Isn't the Only Game in Town

There are other standard forms of advertising that real estate practitioners use: mailings, magazines, and broadcast media.

Some real estate companies publicize important listings with elegant **brochures.** The Iris Group, which specializes in real estate brochures, does magnificent real estate photography, writes text, does layouts, prints, and delivers to its clients brochures to be proud of. An Iris foldover brochure, full color, 1,000 copies, can be had for about $2,000.

Other printing companies do real estate **flyers.** They can produce 1,000 single pages, black-and-white, for less than $300.

Listing agents produce do-it-yourself mailers ad infinitum. By using a computer printer and the neighborhood instant press, do-it-yourselfers can produce fine-looking mailers for a few cents a copy.

Advertising in **real estate magazines** is less expensive than sending out individual mailings and requires less Realtor time since there is no stuffing, licking, or sticking to do; and there's no postage to pay. Some magazines are of coffee-table quality and feature the most expensive estates in the world. A real estate company can advertise a listing in 50,000 issues of a coffee-table magazine for about 5¢ a copy. *Homes and Land* puts out colorful 45-page magazines every two weeks with a local distribution of 20,000 for about 1½¢ a copy. Other magazines, printed on newsprint, with lesser circulations, cost the advertiser about the same per insert as *Homes and Land.* Of course, these approximations can move up or down depending on the quality of the paper stock and photographs, whether the advertising is delivered to the printer camera-ready or not, the size of the advertising piece, circulation figures, and local price customs.

Some of the big boys in the residential real estate business are hawking their wares on TV, on radio, and over computer modems. Radio is the cheapest. For a few hundred dollars a realty company can get itself on the radio. TV and modem advertising may get into thousands of bucks.

Mailings, magazines, TV, and radio are the glamorous kinds of advertising that listing agents crave. Glamour advertising makes sales agents, their realty companies, and their product look important. Glamour advertising has been known to "buy" classy listings. It keeps Godzilla sellers appeased. It keeps sales agents satisfied. Once in a while it attracts clients.

Glamour advertising, generally featuring only one property, costs a bundle per listing compared with classified. But should your company list the White House, George Lucas's Skywalker Ranch, or the isle of Molokai, by all means, cost be damned, use all of the above. Otherwise, don't feel underprivileged if you cannot afford to advertise anywhere but on unglamorous newsprint. You can bring glamour to drab newsprint with your razzle-dazzle ads.

Better Exposure through Classified

Be enthusiastic about classified. It is the real estate professional's loyal friend. Your Sancho Panza. It is there for you day in and day out, the only advertising you can count on to serve your marketing needs 365 days a year. Every realty company can afford classified. Not only can your realty company afford classified, but you can get better exposure through classified, than through any other advertising vehicle, by sheer volume of readership. **Classified Newspaper Advertising Is the Least Expensive Advertising You Can Buy Per Unit Per Consumer.**

No Lag Time

A realty company can get its advertising to several hundred thousand people almost immediately, while other forms of advertising have built-in lag times from four days with do-it-yourself mailings to four months with coffee-table-type magazines. By the time the glamour advertising reaches the public it could be old news.

Classified advertising assures a realty company that the public reads its ads before the advertised listings get sold. A realty company can be sure that price changes are reflected in advertising before it is read. A realty company can be sure that it is not paying big bucks to

6

advertise a listing that has been lost to a competitor (curses!) before the date of publication.

Self-Motivated Readers

Classified advertising offers still another advantage over most other kinds of advertising. Those who read classified have made up their own minds to do so. "Where other advertising seeks out the interested, the interested seek out classified," says Bernard F. Ott, *Springfield Newspapers,* Massachusetts. They open up their newspapers to classified, at their convenience, intent upon finding information about a particular product in which they are already interested. Advertising in classified is like shooting fish in a barrel. Advertising in most other vehicles is like casting into a stream blindfolded with pretty hand-tied flies. Even if the presentation is fantastic, the chance of catching many clients with unsolicited advertising is limited. (How many people who pay attention to unsolicited advertising are currently looking to buy that certain type of property in that particular location at that approximate price?)

Good Ads, But What about Results?

There are many realty companies putting out smart informative classified ads that make the phones ring all right, but not all of them are picking up enough new business from their effective ads. Those offices simply have not prepared to do so:

"Hey, somebody answer the damn phone."

"Where did you see that bungalow ad, ma'am?"

"A guy's calling about Rod's listing. Did he sell it?"

Better-prepared real estate companies are picking up 20 percent, 30 percent, 40 percent, and more of their business from classified alone. These companies are convinced that the classified process is their very own god-given business facilitator. They work it for all it's worth. They are producing good-and-plenty classified ads. Their offices, unlike some less successful offices, are programmed to take full advantage of the responses generated by their good-and-plenty ads. Any ambitious company can do the same once it learns how.

Winning with Classified

The realty offices that are making the most of classified know that ads, written with skill, will inspire potential buyers to contact the real estate agency that wrote them. They know that sellers will be inspired to list with the company that produces the most innovative advertising. They know that the classified advertising that outshines the competitors' will inspire restless agents in other offices to call for employment interviews. They know that consistently clever classified can capture a regular readership for their realty company.

They know that good-and-plenty classified advertising, together with good office preparation and follow-through, can bring to a company public recognition and a position of leadership in the real estate community. They know that good-and-plenty classified advertising, together with good follow-through, can make a realty company wealthy.

It Has Been Done to a Fare-Thee-Well

JM Tayler & Company Realtors, on the San Francisco Peninsula, prospered from a continual flow of new business through its commitment to classified newspaper advertising.

JM Tayler & Company was founded in 1976 in a 90-square-foot office, was undercapitalized, and never employed more than 20 sales agents. Yet within a few years of its founding, JM Tayler & Company became as well known in its community as the giants: Coldwell Banker, Grubb & Ellis, Better Homes, and Prudential. While the giants, in their great big edifice offices, spent millions on all kinds of advertising, this pint-size company put all of its few eggs into classified. The ad copy was showy and plentiful. The sales agents were trained in telephone techniques. Helpmate office systems were developed, fine-tuned, and made gospel.

Under the author's leadership, JM Tayler & Company sales agents earned annual incomes in the six figures. They won awards for excellence. More managers came from JM Tayler & Company, per capita, than from any of the other 200 realty offices in the area. JM Tayler reentry mothers sent their kids to graduate school on their commissions. They funded their own retirement plans. They traveled. Some had face-lifts.

Your Golden Book

In *From Ads to Riches,* you will find the formulae for writing dynamite classified advertising copy. In it you will find the training program that gave the Tayler troops the know-how to respond successfully to inquiries generated by classified advertising. And you will find the office systems that supported the troops in their quests for success.

Are you ambitious? Then read on, join up, and reap **riches**.

To Agents

With a good classified program you can pick up new clients, sitting right there in your office. You can use your company's impressive ad clips as an effective listing tool. You can keep your sellers satisfied and more.

When Tom Goodenough was in his thirties he made a career jump into the field of residential real estate brokerage. He joined a com-

1

pany, near Stanford University, that was well organized and strongly committed to classified advertising. Gung-ho Tom put in for all the agent-on-duty time he could get. He was at the up desk every morning at 7:30 in order to pick up ad calls before the receptionist arrived. The crazy kid hung around long after dark to pick up more. In short order, he had built himself a fat client base off ad calls. Within six months Tom was assistant branch manager. Within two years he owned his own real estate company with three offices. Tom is now on his way to becoming an oil tycoon in Canada.

Who's Gonna Write the Durn Ads?

I beg your pardon. "Who is going to write your dynamite classified real estate advertising?"

Too often, management lets expediency make that decision. In most realty offices, getting the ads out every week is a real pain in the neck. Therefore, the choice is usually a matter of "Who can we get to volunteer?" Little thought is given to quality or to the potential business lost because of lack of quality. The pesky task gets done by:

1. **Newspaper Staff**
2. **The Office Secretary**
3. **Listing Agents**
4. **The Office Manager**
5. **An Advertising Coordinator**
6. **A Copywriter**

1. The classified **newspaper staff** will write ads for its customers. The customer calls up. "Hey, Holly, can you do me up a nice little ad for twenty bucks?" "I'll try, Mr. Ladeback." "Okay," he says. "It's in Teakwood. It's got three bedrooms, two bathrooms, one-car garage, and a basement. I want $125,000 for it." The staff person types it into her computer as he talks. "Sorry, sir. That'll cost $22.50, but I can cut the price if I abbreviate." "Sure, honey. Go ahead. Put it in on Friday." The deed is done, no sweat.

No sweat, no delicious ad calls either. The Ladeback ad comes out, facts correct, just like two dozen other plain vanilla ads written by the newspaper rep for realty customers.

Where's the beef?

Plain vanilla ads

Recommendation: If you are determined to let the newspaper rep do your copywriting, then instruct her to print the headings of your ads in bold type, so that they will stand out from the other vanilla ads:

NEW LISTING
RENT
PROBATE

2. Sometimes the realty **office secretary** writes the company's advertising. She is accurate. She can describe more than Mr. Ladeback's newspaper rep can, because she has a lot of information right there in her listing files. Still she is almost as handicapped as the newspaper rep. She has not seen the properties either. Plus her writing sessions are necessarily interrupted by job responsibilities that have higher priority, like typing up deposit receipts. While realty firm secretaries can be expected to write satisfactory classified ads, they cannot be expected to write blow-your-socks-off ads.

Recommendation: Allow your secretary to inspect your listings. Then give her half a day of solitude each week for her ad-writing session.

3. **Listing agents** have been known to write blow-your-socks-off ads. They should, more often than they do. They've got big commissions at stake.

In most offices, the sales agents write their own ads. A few write blow-your-socks-off ads. Most write vanilla ads. Some write infantile ads too embarrassing to print without major editing. A few forget to write their ads altogether, and have to be chased down on deadline day.

The overall quality is mediocre. The company's advertising looks gobble-de-goop: Group ads do not follow a thought line. The headings jump from architecture to gardens to amenities and back to architecture. The punctuation is not uniform. The size of each ad in the group ad is different.

The classified process puts a strain on the whole office when a dozen or more agents are responsible for turning out their bits and pieces of copy each week. Someone has to chase down forgetful agents. Someone has to approve and edit agents' copy. Someone has to assemble the bits and pieces for the newspapers.

Clever José Dos Ramos, the current owner of JM Tayler & Company Realtors, has established a system that cuts down on office pressure and helps produce better-looking advertising copy. He gives listing agents standard forms to fill out like the one on the next page. The agents are allowed two lines of copy in each ad. Should eager-beaver agents want to submit more lines of copy, they may. But they must pay for the overage themselves. The agents are satisfied and so is José's budget.

Recommendation: Since few sales agents are classified-literate, give your sales force classified training. Your newspaper rep can help you with that. Send your agents to the seminars that newspapers put on for realty folk. Some well-to-do newspapers hire classified gurus like Donn May and Tony Marsella to conduct them. They are not to be missed.

4. Office managers are probably the only people in realty offices who have the know-how and the compulsion to create the dynamite copy that will meet all the objectives of classified real estate advertising:

A. They know every listing.
B. They know the community.
C. They have writing skills.
D. They have the responsibility.

Classified Ad Form

Realty Company_____

Address_____

Phone #_____Fax #_____

Company Agent_____Bill To_____

Newspaper_____

Publication Date_____Under Heading_____

Classification_____Open Home?_____

Headline

___/___/___/___/___/___/___/___/___/___/___/___/___/___/___/___/

___/___/___/___/___/___/___/___/___/___/___/___/___/___/___/___

___/___/___/___/___/___/___/___/___/___/___/___/___/___/___/___

Body Copy

___/___/___/___/___/___/___/___/___/___/___/___/___/___/___/___/

___/___/___/___/___/___/___/___/___/___/___/___/___/___/___/___/

___/___/___/___/___/___/___/___/___/___/___/___/___/___/___/___

___/___/___/___/___/___/___/___/___/___/___/___/___/___/___/___

___/___/___/___/___/___/___/___/___/___/___/___/___/___/___/___

___/___/___/___/___/___/___/___/___/___/___/___/___/___/___/___

___/___/___/___/___/___/___/___/___/___/___/___/___/___/___/___

___/___/___/___/___/___/___/___/___/___/___/___/___/___/___/___/

___/___/___/___/___/___/___/___/___/___/___/___/___/___/___/___

Remarks

_____

_____

_____

_____

Approved By_____

Date_____

2

Office managers have seen every listing and have paid attention to reactions to each. Managers are involved in Realtor board activities. They are involved in community affairs. They have their fingers on the local pulse. They have thousands of megabytes of valuable information in their heads from which they can pull unique, timely, multi-purpose advertising ideas.

Furthermore, managers are experienced authors. Every week they write memos, business letters, contract language, training materials, and sales meeting agendas.

The manager is responsible. No one else in the firm is more concerned with improving bottom line. No one else cares more about the company's public image. No one else will stay up past midnight to write bits and pieces of classified advertising.

However, when management writes the ads, classified is no longer the very affordable marketing tool that it is meant to be. Consider the manager's pay scale. If the manager's hourly wage approximates $40 or $50 an hour, each ad must be priced out $40 or $50 higher than the newspaper's printing charge.

5. **Advertising coordinators** (I call them compilers) are responsible for classified in great big realty companies. The coordinator does not see the properties, nor does he create copy. He adjusts copy written at each individual branch office, where it has been typed on the corporation's fill-in-the-blanks forms.

On his computer in the head office, the coordinator (aka compiler) sorts the ads received from the branch offices. He "cuts" and "pastes." He "deletes." He abbreviates (ouch!), he acronymates (ouch!) in order to comply with his corporation's budget restraints. He fixes the ads together in logical order, much like a tile setter. Then he sends the adjusted, orderly advertising off to the newspapers.

Corporate ads can be big and showy with many listings advertised together in one massive classified ad under the corporation's logo. Such ads are great showcases for multibranch realty firms that offer the public service in several different communities. "Why look for a broker elsewhere?!" is a philosophy that works.

Multioffice realty companies save a lot of money by combining newspaper advertising from all their branches under one account. The more lines of space a contract customer buys, the cheaper each line of copy becomes.

In such cases, where ad copy travels from various offices to the head office, the finished product is more subject to mistakes. It is like the game of "Telephone" kids play at birthday parties. The first kiddy at the table thinks up a phrase, which he whispers into the ear of the kiddy next to him. That kiddy whispers what he's heard into the ear of the kiddy on his other side, and so on around the table until it reaches the last kiddy, who has to stand up and repeat out loud what he's heard. "I heard 'Chocolate Cake,'" he shouts. "But I said 'Baseball Glove!'" shouts the kiddy who started the game. Lots of laughter. The original phrase never travels intact.

I listed an out-of-town house I owned with a branch office of a big company. I unwittingly played the game of Telephone. It was agreed that I would write my own advertising. I pulled together a nice little ad using the form provided. It was important to stress location, the major attribute of the property. So, while I abhor abbreviations, I used them in order to fit the message into the spaces allowed: "Nr schools. Nr rec center. Nr freeway access." The copy traveled from me to the branch office. At the branch office it went to the receptionist for typing, then to the manager for approval. From thence, it traveled via courier to the head office. In the head office it went to the advertising coordinator and/or his assistant. From the advertising coordinator and/or his assistant, it traveled to the newspaper. At the newspaper it traveled from the rep to the print shop. Finally, five days after the journey began, my nice little want ad hit the stands in the Sunday newspaper with a dull thud. The three "Nr's" came out "Nr," "nr," and "NR." And worse, "schools" came out "scls"!

Recommendation: Mistakes are not funny in the grown-up game of business. To avoid mistakes, the coordinator in the head office should fax his final copy back to the branch office for approval before he sends it on to the newspaper.

2

Branch offices suffer another problem when relying upon the head office for advertising. It all takes too long. For example, when the advertising week begins on Monday, the branch must send off its ad copy to the head office the previous Wednesday. Should one of its listings, scheduled to be advertised in the newspaper on Monday, be sold the previous Friday, it runs in the Monday paper anyway. The branch office can't yank it, since the branch office is not the customer of the newspaper, the head office is. If there's a price change later in the week or the seller can't have his house open on Sunday because of measles, tough. The coordinator's finished copy can't be changed.

On the other hand, when an individual realty office employs its own newspapers, the realty office can effect changes and make deletions after copy is in the hands of the newspaper, and with less than twenty-four hours' notice before the paper hits the stands.

Recommendation: Managers of branch offices would be wise to stretch their budgets in order to have their own contracts with newspapers in addition to that of the corporation. While the individual branch office retains exposure in the corporation's showcase ads, the branch is able to control other advertising. By working directly with a newspaper, the branch office can make those last-minute changes. It can advertise a fabulous new listing in the newspaper before it is announced to the Realtor masses on tour day (in hopes of attracting an in-house sale).

As They Say, "I Can't Emphasize Enough"

6. My first and foremost recommendation is that you hire a **copywriter** to write your classified advertising. Unfortunately, few real estate companies do.

Is that because there is no league of classified real estate copywriters out there promoting jobs? Paul Hutchinson, classified editor of the San Francisco Newspaper Agency, suggests that realty companies don't often hire copywriters because they are afraid of the expense. Paul and I could tell them they need not be. A classified real estate copywriter will not be paid nearly as much as an office manager for the same number of ads. He may not be paid as much as the secretary for the same amount of time spent writing.

If copywriters produce ads even only slightly better than vanilla ads, they will pay for their own wages with the extra customers the ads attract. Furthermore, they will relieve the office of pressure on ad day, and free up personnel to do the tasks they do best and for which they were hired.

How Much Is This Gonna Cost Me?

Since there are no guidelines for paying classified real estate advertising copywriters, each manager will have to figure out her own appropriate compensation for the job. Basing it on lines of copy means bookkeeping—not the way to go. Instead, the manager should set a monthly wage based on her estimate of the number of hours of labor involved.

Figure it this way: The company advertises eight times a week. It is assumed that it takes forty-five minutes to an hour to write an ad. Then the sum of eight times forty-five minutes goes in the column. Added to the column is the amount of hours it will take the copywriter to inspect the new listings each week. Added to that is the time the copywriter will spend picking up the weekly ad schedule from the realty office and delivering copy back.

If the copywriter hired is meant to be a "full-service" copywriter, then more hours should be added to the column for time spent doing full-service duty: for typing the copy newspaper-ready, for distributing copy to the manager and listing agents to proof, for stocking the up desk with the weekly advertising schedule and copies of copy, for clipping the ads from the newspapers and pasting them into the ad clip book for posterity, and for approving bills that come in from the newspaper.

When all the hours are added up, the total is multiplied by the hourly wage that management has determined to pay. (You may want to pay your copywriter something more for her mileage and for the use of her personal computer.) Before you make your final decision about what compensation you will offer a copywriter, find out if it is local custom to pay higher wages or lower wages to employees who work at home.

Recommendation: Do have your copywriter work at home. First, desk space is costly. Second, if the copywriter works at home instead of in your office she is not so apt to be harassed by aggressive sales agents who push for more coverage than your budget policy allows. For the same reason, you do not want to give the job to one of your agents, as long as the agent is still engaged in brokerage. Get the whole function out of the place. This will have a calming effect on your office.

Recruiting a Copywriter

Where to find a copywriter, since there is no league of classified real estate advertising copywriters to go to? One cannot recruit a classified real estate copywriter from the local university. Universities do not give degrees in classified real estate advertising. Government labor departments and commercial employment agencies list no such category. Therefore, realty offices must seek elsewhere, through:

1. **Classified Advertising**
2. **Sales Agents**
3. **Schools**
4. **Writers' Clubs**
5. **Society Editors**

1. Place a want ad in classified:

(Ask your classified rep if she has a crony who would like the job.)

2. Residential real estate **sales agents** know everyone in town. Involve your staff in the search.

3. Check with the local **schools**. Teachers write. Maybe teachers will recommend graduates. (Do not hire a student. Students are here today and gone tomorrow. You want a copywriter who will be a permanent member of your growth team.)

4. Do not be intimidated by **writers' clubs**. Most published authors make less than the minimum hourly wage for their skilled work. "Copywriter, Advertising" would look good on any writer's bio.

5. Your local **society editor** is a very likely source. Every business day society editors receive bundles of press releases from volunteers who want free newspaper coverage for their charities. Some of the volunteers' releases get printed. The volunteers who wrote them get hooked on the excitement of seeing their words in print. Some might love to go "pro." Ask your society editor for introductions.

I was one of those volunteers, doing publicity for Crippled Children's Auxiliary, when my friend Bette Chapin and her broker, Bill Wright, recruited me as copywriter. It seems that their realty company was in mutiny over its vanilla ads, its inconsistent advertising, and the turmoil it was causing in the workplace. Having been a real estate consumer, I managed to pound out better than vanilla ads, after the children were put to bed, on my secondhand Royal, a relic from the Los Angeles School District. How I could have used this guidebook and a computer!

Interview Time!

2

Your networking has born fruit. Your recruiting efforts have brought a couple of would-be copywriters to your office. Don't be concerned, for the time being, if one arrives dressed "Berkeley" in caftan and prayer beads and another in tennis whites. Which one will you choose? The candidate you hire is the one who is:

1. Local
2. Involved
3. Responsible
4. A Reader

1. You want a copywriter who is a **local** resident. Better still, you want someone who has lived locally for a long time so that she can use local history as well as local awareness in her ads.

ON STONEHEDGE ROAD
where polo ponies paraded
in the olden days

A newcomer could err. A gorgeous condo complex was built on the site of an old Red Cross headquarters south of San Francisco. A newcomer might, logically, describe the location that way, not realizing that the "townies" had grieved when the charming Red Cross landmark was torn down a few years back.

2. The copywriter you choose should be **involved** in the community. Interesting, appreciated copy comes from knowledge of local happenings. Super, if the candidate serves on the hospital board, if her husband plays golf, if her children are enrolled in local schools, if her mother is a member of Senior Focus:

NEAR THE PGA-RATED GOLF COURSE

ON YOUR WAY TO THE SCHOOL FAIR

3. It takes a little digging to find out if the candidate is **responsible.** While creativity is important to exceptional copywriting, so is dependability. You don't want a laid-back *artiste* who is deaf to deadlines, is not prone to double-check facts, and doesn't get around to returning your calls in a timely fashion. Those who refer candidates ought to be able to screen for you.

4. A person who writes good advertising is a good **reader.** A lot of good classified ads have been pulled from children's books:

Christopher Robin Cottage

A Secret Garden

Little Women

And from the classics:

Juliet's Balcony

Milton's Paradise *Found*

Tale of Two Cities

Ask your interviewees what newspapers and periodicals they read. Do they open their junk mail? It is clever to hitch a ride on the big boys' advertising:

White Flower Days (Macy's)

Promise Her Anything, But Give Her... (Arpège)

***Big Blue* Means Service** (IBM)

2

Where Service Is State of the Art (Circuit City)

Move with the Name You Know (Mayflower Transit)

(Incidentally, if your future copywriter uses a slogan unaltered, better have her identify the company that owns it.)

Habitual readers automatically collect ideas and vocabulary that are useful in creating innovative advertising.

If a candidate meets the criteria in the interview, move on to the job description. As with most people queried about their opinions of classified, your candidate will assume that the sole purpose of classified real estate advertising is to sell. Set her straight. You expect your classified advertising to "sell" real estate, of course, by first making the phones ring. She must understand that your advertising is meant, also, to attract sellers who are searching classified for a firm to represent them in the marketing of their properties. It is meant to impress real estate licensees who are searching for a firm to join, by demonstrating a strong advertising program. Tell her that you want your classified advertising to spread the word that yours is a realty firm with flair. And that it is your wish to develop a loyal readership that will "talk up" the company in the community.

In the interview, you will also discuss previewing new listings, newspaper deadlines, quantity of advertising, and the copywriter's salary.

If these discussions produce mutual satisfaction, then take your candidate to see one of your listings. Let her snoop around. Then bring her back to the office. Put her in the conference room and have her **write** an ad or two on the property she just saw. If the ads are okay, hire her!

Close Her

Before you shake hands, have her read a simple employment agreement. You can adapt the language from the standard independent contractor contract that your sales agents sign when you hire them. Make note of the salary, the weekly advertising schedule (subject to change at the manager's option), termination routine, and anything else that is pertinent to establishing complete understanding of the mutual obligations. Be sure that your written agreement includes the following language:

> All written materials submitted to_____(company name) by _____(copywriter's name), whether published or not, shall immediately become the sole and permanent property of _____(company), and shall not be copied, reproduced, quoted in any way, in part or whole without advance written permission of the company signed by the owner and/or manager of _____ (company). This condition of the foregoing agreement is irrevocable.

It could come to pass that your copywriter is stolen away by a competitor. You don't want to read the dynamite copy you paid for printed in the newspaper above your competitor's logo.

"Oh, By the Way..."

Quite often, just before a new hireling puts her signature to the employment agreement, she announces that she has a vacation planned. You may respond that the company can handle that. The copywriter will be required to prepare two weeks of advertising prior to departure. During her absence, management will assign someone to write up new listings and "opens" not yet scheduled.

Writing School?

For sure, your new copywriter has not made an in-depth study of classified real estate advertising. She requires teaching. Don't panic. You won't have to conduct writing school. Just give your copywriter *From Ads to Riches*. After she's read it, send her to the newspaper for instruction. The classified rep will be primed to tell her about:

1. Schedules/deadlines
2. Form in which copy is to be presented
3. Understanding the rate sheet
4. Deciphering newspaper bills, if it's her job to approve them
5. The newspaper's office hours
6. How to make last-minute changes
7. Discount deals
8. Restrictions on copy language

In-House Training

Have the secretary show the new copywriter around the office. Have her show the copywriter how to use the phones, how to operate the copier and fax machine, where to find supplies. Have the secretary show her where to find the *Ad Clip Book,* the *Ad Schedule Book,* the *In-House Listing Book,* and the *Multiple Listing Service Book.* All of these will be used when writing the ads. (The *MLS Book* is not supposed to be seen by non-Realtors. The ball is in your ethics court.) After a trial period, the secretary can give your new copywriter a key to the office and explain the security system.

Now the manager takes over. He assigns a message slot to the copywriter. He tells her that this is where to find the updated rosters, the up-to-the-minute listing inventory, and communications from the newspaper. Here she will also receive notes from management: "Please advertise this listing on Tuesday," "The Hacienda ad pulled 12 calls." She will receive notes from the sales agents as well: "Thanks for the great ad," "The seller insists that we call his back porch 'The Lanai.'"

The manager opens the listing file drawer. The copywriter may go into the files anytime for information. The manager explains how to read the showing instructions featured in the profile sheets, because individual appointments may be needed to see listings. Emphasize that the contents of those files are confidential. Housing is a universal topic of conversation. Warn that friends may quiz her about company listings once they know she has joined the "racket." This is one situation where "I dunno; it's not my job" is the response of choice. Better still, the copywriter could give the name of the curious cat, with his phone number, to the appropriate listing agent.

Provide your copywriter with blank business cards on which to type her name. The public expects real estate people to present cards when entering a residence. You'll order cards with her name and "Advertising Director" printed on them after you know she's going to stay aboard. "Advertising Director" looks good. It tells the public that yours is not a kitchen-table operation. Consider sending out announcements, for PR value, introducing your new advertising director.

Somewhere in your training, you may want to address that sensitive subject of dress code. Tell your new copywriter that everyone is expected to dress in suitable business attire when representing the company.

One day, after she's proved her worth, you may want to provide your copywriter with a home computer and printer. Your new classified advertising campaign, together with your new copywriter, is going to bring you many more listings. Either you will have to increase your copywriter's salary for the extra work resulting, or you could buy her that computer and printer, which will enable her to write about your increased inventory in the same time it took her before to hand write or to type copy on her secondhand Royal.

2

To Agents

Even if you have been gifted with an honest-to-gosh copywriter, don't snooze. Be responsible to your clients. Stick lots of helpful hints about your listings into the copywriter's message slot.

If you are not gifted with a copywriter and still have to write your own ads, then do so with flair. Once a week go to a quiet corner. Take off your Realtor's pin. Put on your green eyeshade. And be a professional copywriter for just that hour or two. Create dynamite classified advertising that will make you and your company proud, and that will make your sellers ecstatic over the superb marketing techniques of their incredible listing agent.

Ready, Get Set, Write!

3

"Copy writers all: Now hear this. You are to proceed to your battle stations. Assemble your weapons. Make ready for combat." The writing session is about to commence.

You have before you:

1. **The Open Home Schedule**
2. **The Current Inventory List**
3. **The In-House Listing Book**
4. **The Multiple Listing Book**
5. **The Ad Clip Book**

(Agents who write ads only about their own listings do not need to assemble all these "weapons.")

Scan the inventory list. How many properties will have to fit into the ad schedule? Which properties get priority treatment? Which properties will look good together in a combo ad? Which are the toughies?

How Big Is the Baby? So Big!

3

The open home ad is the biggest baby of the week. The size of the others will be decided as each is checked off the inventory list.

What determines the size of the ads? The budget determines first. Next, the importance of a particular ad is the **determinator**. (The manager may not be willing to spring for a $200 ad on a $25,000 loft.) Third, the design of the ad determines. (A one-column ad with stars could be a real hot dog on Fourth of July.)

The column width influences the number of words and size type used. A two-column ad, or "two by," is two and one-half inches wide, give or take an eighth of an inch. It is at least two inches deep. A "one by" is one and three-sixteenths inches wide and can be as thin as one-fourth of an inch deep.

Two-column ads are more expensive than one-column ads. The cost of each varies according to the column inch. The cost of ads also varies from newspaper to newspaper; usually the higher the circulation of the newspaper the higher the rate. (Your newspaper will give you a rate card that gives measurements, costs, and circulation figures.) Most realty companies find it too expensive to print two-column ads in newspapers with a circulation over 100,000. A two-and-one-half-inch-by-three-inch ad will not pull as well in a newspaper with a 5,000 circulation as will a two or three liner in a newspaper with a circulation of 100,000:

> Estate: 22 rooms.
> Lake Forest. $2,000,000.

> CUTIE PIE
> White Picket Fence.
> 2 Bedrooms. Marin. $80,000.

Two- and three-line ads

Instructions to the newspaper concerning size, type size, spacing, and the date the ad is to appear, are noted on the same page as the copy to which it refers. The copy itself is always typed double or triple spaced, one ad to each piece of paper.

3

ONE COL.

TWO COL.

THREE COL.

FOUR COL.

FIVE COL.

SIX COL.

SEVEN COL.

1″

2″

3″

4″

5″

6″

7″

8″

9″

10″

Column inch scale

NOT SHOWN: 8, 9 and 10 column classified measurements:
8 column ..... 10⅜ inches
9 column ..... 11¹¹⁄₁₆ inches
10 column .... 13 inches

3 Write Sunday "Opens" First

Always begin your writing session with the Sunday open home ad.

Previously, your open home ad format was established with the newspaper, a format that is automatically repeated every time your company places an open home ad in the paper. This ad, bigger than your weekday ads, will be a "display ad" since the company logo appears at the bottom or at the top of the copy. (A logo is not required, but is highly advisable.)

Recommendation: Unless yours is a "showcase" ad with many properties advertised therein, it is best to locate the logo, together with the company phone number (prominent) and address, at the bottom. You are not selling a real estate company, you are selling real estate. **Feature the real estate.**

If your logo, which you use on signs and stationery, is complicated, you may want to go back to your graphic designer to have him design a simplified version of your logo for use in the newspaper.

Graphic designer Jerry Reis did design work for the San Francisco Museum of Modern Art and for JM Tayler & Company Realtors. The logo he designed for JM Tayler & Company featured a heather plant, roots exposed. The inspiration was taken from the founder's Scottish heritage. The logo was much admired (except by ex-husbands of the firm who called it the "weed" or the "pot plant"). It was somewhat complicated and delicate. Sometimes the newspaper print shop would over-ink, and our delicate heather logo would become a blob.

Heather logo with and without blob

Logos can be tricky and they stay with us forever. A multioffice giant has a handsome logo that depicts a house and two trees. The trees are solid lime green circles with sticklike trunks. Agents who work for that company are called the "lollipop kids."

If your company name is so long that it has to be reduced down to eight-point type in order to fit the line, then cut out words and heavy up the type. Do not fail to identify, however, that the subject property is being advertised by a company, or individual, engaged in the business of real estate brokerage. Identification can be "Broker," "R. E.," "Realtors," "Agt," or a reproduction of the official Realtor insignia: ®. The law is not precise. The National Association of Realtors, however, is precise when addressing its membership on the matter of identification of advertisers:

> *Realtors shall not advertise or permit any person employed by or affiliated with them to advertise listed property without disclosing the name of the firm.*
> —*Code of Ethics and Standards of Practice,* Article 19-4

You will be placing your ad on the newspaper's separate page devoted to the "Open Home Guide" or the "Sunday Open Home Tour." Nevertheless, print your own announcement at the top of your ad as it is to appear in newsprint:

OPEN SUN 1:30–4:30

Remember: The object of an open home ad is to get people to visit "opens." Tell your readers, crystal clear, where the properties are **and how to get there.**

In your open ad, group your properties under the name of the towns in which they are located. If all the properties are in the same town or city, then the properties are grouped under category names fixed by the newspaper, such as tract names or subdivision names, or under descriptive terms such as "East side," "South of Market," or "Country Property."

3

34

The body copy starts with the address of each property. Somewhere, either following the address near the top, or at the bottom, in parentheses or in smaller type, put the directions to the property. Where the property is really off the beaten track or difficult to find, you may need to write a whole line of directions: "from Jones & Vallejo, drive up ramp, turn right on Florence." Delete amenities, if you must, to accommodate adequate directions. Not every Lookie-Louie carries a map in his glove compartment.

Since addresses are the attention grabbers in open home ads, you will not need to give other headlines center stage as well. Rather than placing another headline by itself on yet another line, begin your descriptive copy with a heading in caps, running it on the same line as the body copy that follows. Keep these inside headlines in the same family throughout the entire ad. Repeat architecture or adjectives in the same sequence. Repeat your punctuation when describing each property. Keep to a pattern. Don't write about the bedrooms and bathrooms of one home, then omit the bathrooms of the next. Give each property you advertise in the open home guide the same number of lines. Your ad will look ever so "J. Walter Thompson."

Monday through Saturday Ads

After the big open homes ad is done, you will attack the Monday through Saturday ads. Begin by writing ads on brand-new listings. You will probably schedule them to run in the paper as soon as possible. Brokers always want to attract ad calls before new listings are made known to the other realty offices. Mind the days. Some days pull better than others. Fridays are usually good days to advertise important listings, because serious lookers turn out on weekends.

Keep surveying your inventory list as you write. It is easy to run out of days and have unadvertised listings left over if you don't keep track.

Your company may be committed to advertising each listing at least four times a month, the right idea. With an inventory of thirty listings and only eight days of advertising available, it is a challenge

3

to accommodate the commitment. It can be done, provided one person is assigned to write all the ads for the week:

1. The open home group ads wipe several off the list in one day.

2. A few properties have received double advertising the week before. So they may be omitted the coming week. (Perhaps the newspaper automatically runs opens on Saturdays as well as Sundays. Perhaps all Monday or Wednesday classifieds are automatically repeated in satellite newspapers.)

3. The copywriter writes a combo ad grouping similar properties: All have swimming pools. All are ranch style. All are co-ops:

POOLS, POOLS, POOLS

CONDO COLLECTION

HOMES NEAR SCHOOLS

CONTEMPOS!

4. The copywriter writes a combo ad, grouping dissimilar leftovers:

Variety Pak

Potpourri

FULL-SERVICE BROKER

5. The copywriter does several scatter ads using mismatched leftovers.

Scatter ads, six or seven inexpensive little fellows, are effective. The realty company's name pops up all over the classified page. Scatter ads are best printed apart under the newspaper's separate categories.

COZY
COTTAGES

TWO COZY COTTAGES on one Sunny Burlingame lot. One cute "Country Ranch" with 2 bedrooms. The other, a shiny white "Country Victorian" with 2 bedrooms. Buy both for $300,000.

J M TAYLER & CO.
Realtors   342-9252
100 El Camino, Burl

STORYBOOK
HOUSE

In a Fairytale. Flower-Bower Garden. 4 Bedrooms, Dining Room. $285,000.

J M TAYLER & CO.
Realtors   342-9252
100 El Camino, Burl.

TRADITIONAL

Impressive Living Room, Dining Room, Dens, 3 Bedrooms, Favorite North Burlingame Neighborhood. Off Easton. $575,000.

J M TAYLER & CO.
Realtors   342-9252
100 El Camino, Burl.

DASHING
DUPLEX

In Burlingame. Quite modern. 4 years old. 1 Bedroom Each, Fireplaces Each. $300,000.

J M TAYLER & CO.
Realtors   342-9252
100 El Camino, Burl.

Scatter ads

(They lose impact if they abut.) The paper may separate sections in columns according to town or area and/or according to: Vacant Land, Condominiums/Townhouses, Single Family Dwellings, Investment Property, Horse Property, Shared Housing. (Variety pak ads and scatter ads are most often written at midnight…)

In the 1970s, a real estate company with headquarters in Belmont, California, was in the habit of publishing only scatter ads. Every day of the week it would print up to a dozen scatter ads in the local newspaper. The copy was dumb. Nevertheless, the company did 75 percent of its business from classified.

Heads Up for Headlines!

The headline is the most important part of any classified ad. If the headline doesn't catch readers' attention, the body copy doesn't have a chance.

Headlines should be printed in the boldest type possible. Bold type gives bland words drama. Try to fill the entire width of the column with the headline. Write instructions on the copy page you send to the newspaper. "Headline: 24-Point Type All Caps."

Headlines may contain only one word:

OLÉ

BARGAIN

RARE!

Headlines need not be only one line long. Headlines with two or more lines attract more attention than one-line headlines:

SKI ASPEN?
WEAR ARMANI?
FLY THE CONCORDE?
WANT A PENTHOUSE?

5 MIN. TO DEPOT
10 MIN. TO BALLPARK
15 MIN. TO FINANCIAL DISTRICT

ALPHABET
SOUP

(Begin the first line of body copy with A,
the next with B, the next with C, etc.)

When Dynamite Headlines Elude Us

Homes have character just as people have character. Headlines focus on the character of the property. They may focus on the character of the people who will fit the character of the property. Some

CLASSIFIED TYPEFACES

CLASSIFIED MARKETPLACE	**No.1 Type Capital** 25 Letters and Spaces
classified marketplace	**No. 1 Type Lower Case** 25 Letters and Spaces
CLASSIFIED MARKETPL	**No. 10 Type Capital** 19 Letters and Spaces
classified marketplace	**No. 10 Type Lower Case** 22 Letters and Spaces
CLASSIFIED MARK	**No. 14 Type Capital** 15 Letters and Spaces
classified marketp	**No. 14 Type Lower Case** 17 Letters and Spaces
CLASSIFIED M	**No. 18 Type Capital** 12 Letters and Spaces
classified mar	**No. 18 Type Lower Case** 14 Letters and Spaces
CLASSIFIE	**No. 24 Type Capital** 9 Letters and Spaces
classified	**No. 24 Type Lower Case** 11 Letters and Spaces
CLASSIFI	**No. 30 Type Capital** 8 Letters and Spaces
classified	**No. 30 Type Lower Case** 10 Letters and Spaces
CLASSI	**No. 36 Type Capital** 6 Letters and Spaces
classifi	**No. 36 Type Lower Case** 8 Letters and Spaces
CLAS	**No. 48 Type Capital** 4 Letters and Spaces
classi	**No. 48 Type Lower Case** 6 Letters and Spaces

Examples of type size

properties appear to lack any character whatsoever. In that case, the copywriter digs deeper. The present owner must have found something to love about it, or he wouldn't have bought it. Maybe the only thing to recommend the home is a six-burner Wolfe range (which is to remain on the premises, if it is mentioned). Now you've got yourself a headline for that boring house:

CHEF'S KITCHEN

When you check over your finished ads, you might find your best headlines buried in the body copy. If so, move them.

When Inspiration Eludes Us

Every realty office gets it share of boring listings. Some okay listings hang around forever and become boring with time. "Boy, is this a tired listing." Sometimes copywriters get writer's block and need help getting started. So here is a list of headline categories. It will help jog the writer's mind when paralyzed by the block. Paste it in your copy book.

1. **Location**
2. **Architecture**
3. **Special Amenities**
4. **Children**
5. **Gardening**
6. **Hobbies**
7. **Sports**
8. **Holidays**
9. **Weather**
10. **Colors**
11. **Book and Song Titles**
12. **Money**

13. **Snob Appeal**
14. **Sex Appeal**

1. **Location** is the most important criterion in buyers' search for real estate. While specific addresses are given only in open home ads, nonspecific location identification attracts attention in other ads:

ON TELEGRAPH HILL

BY A TROUT STREAM

ALONG THE SILVERADO TRAIL

ON SEABURY ROAD

5TH AVE BROWNSTONE

BELOVED BETHESDA

You may want to put the specific name of the town in your headline, if the town is particularly desirable. You should put the name of the town or city somewhere in your ad if the town name does not clearly head the column or section in which your ad is to appear.

2. Architecture draws mental pictures:

STONE TUDOR

PUEBLO STYLE

COUNTRY CONTEMPO

3

RAMBLIN' RANCH

SCOTTISH COACH HOUSE

PAINTED LADY
(Another name for Victorian in San Francisco)

It is not necessary to draw the whole structure. Significant parts make mental pictures too:

CARRIAGE LAMPS & SHUTTERS

TILE ROOF, WROUGHT IRON

NEW ORLEANS BALCONIES

THATCHED ROOF

WHITE PILLARS

BROWN SHINGLED

ADOBE

3. Whet appetites with **special amenities** in headlines:

CRYSTAL/MARBLE/MIRRORS

FOUR-CAR GARAGE

OFF-STREET PARKING

BARN & PADDOCK

BUILT-INS:
STEREO, VACUUM, SECURITY, INTERCOM

HUGE ATTIC!

4. People with **children** have more entries on their want lists than most other home buyers:

WALK TO SCHOOL

KIDDY-CARE FENCING

FIVE BEDROOMS !!!

ATTIC PLAYROOM

KICK-THE-CAN CUL-DE-SAC

AU PAIR'S ROOM

5. Gardening is the number-one pastime in the United States. Use it:

ROSES, AZALEAS, RHODIES

FRESH LAVENDER, LUV

NO CRABGRASS HERE!

GREENHOUSE & POTTING SHED

HORTICULTURIST'S DELIGHT

VEGGIE GARDEN

3

6. People in the United States spent a lot of time on their **hobbies**:

HOBBY ROOM

FITNESS ROOM

SEWING ROOM

BUILDER'S WORKSHOP

ART STUDIO

POET'S CORNER

7. Americans are **sports** minded:

10 MIN. TO STADIUM

NEAR ICE RINK

2 POOLS, 2 TENNIS COURTS

BOAT DOCK

HEY, SKI BUMS!

8. **Holidays** come along just when tired copywriters need ideas the most:

2 TURKEY, 4 PIE SIZE KITCHEN

16 FT. TREE WILL FIT

COMIN' PDQ!
MEMORIAL DAY BBQ!

DEAREST DADDY'S DAY

HOPPIN' DOWN THE BUNNY TRAIL

WEE GHOSTS & GOBLINS

LUCK O' THE IRISH

GUNG HAY FAT CHOY

(lovey-dovey stuff on Valentine's Day)

9. "Everybody talks about the **weather,** but no one does anything about it." Do something about it in your ads:

SNOWPLOW INCLUDED
(Use only in winter)

WHAT A SCORCHER!!

SPLISH SPLASH

SHADE OF THE OLD OAK TREE
(Use swimming and shade only in spring and summer)

**RAIN, RAIN GO AWAY
COME AGAIN SOME OTHER DAY**

**HATE CLEANIN' GUTTERS? HATE RAKIN' LEAVES?
HATE SHOVELIN' SNOW?**
(Use in a condo or co-op ad after a storm)

10. **Colors** have psychological and esthetic appeal. Use colors that are fashionable in your area now. In Northern California yellow houses sell fast, while blue houses can take a long time to sell. In the fifties, brown wooden contemporaries were all the rage out West.

Now brown contempos have lost favor except in the mountains. In Camden, Maine, white is too fashionable. It won't attract much attention in a headline because there is so much of it: white houses, white churches, white sails, and white lilacs.

BEHIND THE RED DOOR

GREEEEEN
(on St. Patrick's Day)

YELLOW ROSE OF TEXAS, IN TULSA

PINK? YES, PINK!

WHITE COLONIAL
Follow that headline in the body copy with:

WHITE picket fence
WHITE magnolias
WHITE bathrooms
WHITE carpets

11. Copywriters have home libraries from whence they can extract headline **book titles**:

IN SEARCH OF EXCELLENCE

GREAT EXPECTATIONS

THE HOUSE OF SEVEN GABLES
(maybe only two)

GOD'S LITTLE ACRE *Approximately*

A YEAR IN PROVENCE
(French architecture)

RIVER RUNS THROUGH IT

JOY LUCK *HOUSE*

Popular **song titles** can be lifted for headlines:

UNFORGETTABLE

'S WONDERFUL

RHAPSODY IN BLUE

LA BOHÈME

ON THE SUNNY SIDE OF THE STREET

ON THE ROAD AGAIN
(owner transferred)

Years ago, there was a broker in San Mateo County, California, who had a large sheet music collection. All of his headlines were taken from song titles. His classified readership was as large as his collection.

12. **Money** is in every classified reader's mind. Trade on that:

BIG HOUSE, SMALL PRICE

ONLY 50 K!
(use price in headlines only with real cheapies)

OWNER FINANCING
or
ASSUMABLE LOAN
(when mortgage money is scarce or expensive)

3

REFI,
INVEST PROCEEDS

(follow headline with rentable properties)

CHEEP! CHEEP! (This little chickie is CHEEP.)

$5,000 MOVES YOU IN

(this headline always pulls buyers for real estate columnist/lawyer/ investor Robert Bruss; it refers to lease/option terms)

13. People say that they cannot abide **snob appeal.** Then how come so many "snob-snobs" read the society columns? Why do they read magazines like *Architectural Digest, Vanity Fair, W,* and *Town and Country?* How does one explain the popularity of TV shows like *Lifestyles of the Rich and Famous, Dallas,* and *Falcon Crest?* We all have dreams. Snob appeal ads pull:

MANSION ROW

JAGUAR JUNCTION

PRINCESS DI SLEPT HERE

FORMER SWISS CONSULATE

Locating a property near that of a celebrity always creates interest for the property:

ON JACKIE O'S BLOCK

While Bing Crosby owned a home at Pebble Beach, California, Realtors were bugged by visiting golfers who wanted directions so that they could drive by "Der Bingle's" house.

While a celebrity's name in an ad is sure to grab attention, use it with discretion. If the celebrity has moved from the neighborhood,

Trader Vic's estate for sale

it's okay to mention his name. If the celebrity is still in residence and you still think it advantageous to use his name in an ad, be sure to get the celebrity's permission first before putting his name in print.

JM Tayler & Company Realtors listed Trader Vic's California estate. We were given permission, by his widow, to use the famous restaurateur's name in our classified advertising. The editorial departments of two newspapers picked up on it. As a result of printing the Trader's name in our ads, the listing received some fabulous free press on the editorial pages!

Intellectual snob appeal pulls. Comedian Mort Sahl draws crowds with intellectually elite humor. Audiences love Sahl's sophisticated jokes made at the expense of politicians, financial leaders, and corporations. Even when they don't understand the jokes, the crowds are proud to be a part of Sahl's intellectually elite audience.

Make use of snobbish intellectualism in headlines. Use "Fortune 500" language:

ASK ERNST & YOUNG

LEADING GAINERS

THE FRANKLIN/TEMPLETON GROUP

3

Use elite places:

CAP D'ANTIBES, *USA*

HYANNIS PORT *WEST*

Flatter readers by using foreign words in your headlines:

C'EST MAGNIFIQUE!

MOLTA BELLA!

MI CASA, SU CASA

NOUVEAU LISTING

Some readers may not understand all your elitist or foreign words, but they will like being in your audience anyway:

ROSE-COVERED BELVEDERE

BOLECTION MOLDING

ANTEBELLUM

Better note definitions in the *Ad Schedule Book* on the up desk in case an ad caller asks the floor person for a translation.

14. **Sex appeal** is used to market everything from automobiles to cosmetics to packaged bread. Use sex appeal, as Letitia Baldridge would say, "with taste." Sex reported as romance is always tasteful:

MOONBEAMS & BLACK SATIN

ROMANTIC!

HONEYMOONERS' HIDEAWAY

JE T'AIME

The newspaper will disallow:

BACHELOR'S PAD

SINGLES' SOLUTION

SEX AND THE SINGLE GIRL

Seeking GWM with No Inhibitions

You may get away with:

BIKINI TIME!

SKINNY-DIPPING

THE KING IS IN THE ALTOGETHER
tanning his bod

CHATTERLEY'S CABIN

MADONNA'S CHOICE?

TU ES CAPITEUSE

PEEK-A-BOO

Peter Piper Picked a Peck of Pickled Peppers

Headlines are quite quotable when the first letters of key words are the same:

3

PAT'S PAD

LEISURE LODGE

CONNOISSEUR CONDOMINIUMS

BOTANICAL BUNGALOW

SHUTTERS, SHINGLES, & SHAKES

CUNNING CO-OP

FOG CITY FLAT

TIP TOP TOWNHOUSE

Picture the Place

Think of your ad as a billboard which must immediately catch the reader's eye or be missed completely, and you'll understand the importance of your ad's first word or two. Since you can't include a picture of the place in your ad, the descriptive words you use have to conjure up the most appealing picture possible. Words like "sparkling," "just painted," "quiet," "super clean," "cozy," "super big," and "quaint" all create positive, pleasant pictures in readers' minds. They'll want a closer look.

So writes Leigh Robinson in his blockbuster book, *Landlording*.

Into the Body Copy

The body copy takes its direction from the headline. Your tantalizing headline grabs the reader's attention and makes her want to read on. Do not disappoint your reader by abandoning the thought that attracted her. It's best to start the body copy with a word or phrase that reinforces the message of the headline:

HAWAIIAN HALE
Palm Trees and Tiki Torches...

CHALET
On Bear Mountain, shuttle to slopes...

NEAR SHOPS
Five & Dime, The Gap, Penney's...

Next go on to essentials. Classified real estate experts instruct that the price, the location, bedrooms, and bathrooms are of first importance and must be addressed in every good ad. Next in importance may be the dining room, the family room, and the garage.

Copywriters may need to create their own lists of essentials. While the above essentials are important when advertising most residential properties, tain't necessarily so in every case. Should you be advertising a five-bedroom house having only one bathroom, mentioning that one bathroom could be a turnoff. In Manhattan, there aren't any residential garages, except in extravagant buildings, so one seldom sees parking advertised. To a rancher or a farmer, water and acreage are far more important than housing. Be aware. Know the essential needs of prospects in your market area.

Follow your essentials with amenities. The amenities can be decor, conveniences, other rooms, esthetics, and descriptions.

Sometimes the amenities are just tag-alongs, not dramatic:

Fresh paint

Attic

Full basement

Mud room

Root cellar

Vacant

Other times, the amenities make dramatic closings:

Brand New Listing!

DAIRY CLEAN

OWNER FINANCING

Winner of Garden Award!

Dramatic closings look more dramatic when given exclams (exclamation points) or printed all in caps (capital letters).

Location makes an important closing:

Off Skyline Blvd.

ACROSS FROM PARK

By Madison Bridge!

Not to worry if the size of an ad will not allow for a closing language. Just be certain that the essentials are included somewhere in the copy. You can count on price always being an attention-grabbing closing.

The best place for that all-important price is in a spot where it is obvious. It must not be buried in the copy. (Isn't hunting for price in a four-page mailer, typically advertising a seminar, a real pain?) At the end of the body copy, before the realty company name, is the best place to print the price. A couple of bullets (periods) stuck in front of the price makes it stand out. The name of the company and the company's phone number, prominently displayed, following the price, printed in different type, also make the price stand out.

Out, Out Damned Abbreviations!

Avoid abbreviations and acronyms like the plague. It is a damned impertinence to obligate readers of classified to spend time deciphering. Besides, abbreviations and acronyms aren't as pretty as words. (St., Ave., Blvd., Rd., Ln., and Ct. are permissible, of course.)

Power Punctuation and Spatial Gymnastics

Use punctuation for emphasis:

!!SCARCE AS HEN'S TEETH!!

Use punctuation and white space to separate parts of the copy: interior from exterior, amenities from rooms, price from body copy. Underline. Use a blank line of space between the headline and the body copy. Don't scrunch them together. Proper spacing makes the text easier to read.

Signal the Newspaper

It's all right to make up words as long as you alert the newspaper that they aren't mistakes:

ENGLISH-ISH

PULEEZE

DEE-VINE!

RICHIE RANCHIE

HOWS 'N' GARDIN

3

Washington Post columnist George Will is famous for making up words. Foreign words and weird words are fun, but they can drive your classified rep crazy. Let your rep know, with a note on the copy page, that you actually intended to write those weird words.

Don't Give Away the Store

Don't pontificate even if you have a fat advertising budget, even if your manager wants all two-column ads (that'll be the day!), even if there are two dozen incredible features to the house. Save some goodies for the next ad. Readers of classified have no interest in wading through a lot of rhetoric. Certainly you do not want to satisfy your potential buyers' curiosity altogether in a newspaper ad, or else they won't need to contact the realty office to get more information.

Zealous sellers may want their entire house reproduced in toto in each classified ad. "You didn't mention the microwave." (Oh, give me a break.) Someone should inform such sellers that you don't buy a dog and bark for it.

Omit the "Negs"

Don't write negative copy. It doesn't pull. Americans buy in celebration. Shopping is happy time. Think of all those cheerful faces in the shopping mall. Don't turn your potential buyers glum. If you do, they will not feel inspired to pick up the phone.

Don't recall tragic events: "Survived the Earthquake," "Withstood the Hurricane." Don't attempt to threaten prospects into action: "Interest Rates Going Up," "Prices Going Up." No sad cries for help: "Owner Desperate," "Lost Job, Must Sell."

An Exception, Old Chap

From 1950 to 1971 London estate agent Roy Brooks wrote outrageous, funny, painfully accurate, *negative* advertisements that disparaged the properties he was hired to sell and sometimes the people who hired him to sell them. The Brits loved the ads and loved him for them.

"He was most definitely an odd ball, but a charming and amusing one. Every Sunday that I was in the UK, or abroad if I could find a decent English newspaper, I would always search for his adverts so that I could enjoy his wit, even if I did not avail myself of his 'special offers,'" said Stirling Moss, international race car driver. Here are some excerpts from Brooks's "adverts":

BROTHEL IN PIMLICO

FILTHY OLD HOUSE—FASHIONABLE CHELSEA

ONE OF THE FILTHIEST HOUSES
I'VE SEEN FOR A LONG TIME

WE ALWAYS THOUGHT
"NOBODY LIVES SOUTH OF THE RIVER"

FASHION DESIGNER & Van Driver offers her amusing little MEWS COTTAGE, decor somewhat party-worn, but some interesting graffiti.

WILL ANYONE TAKE PITY ON
A NASTY OLD HOUSE

A SHABBY OLD HOUSE NR. CAMDEN TOWN

FASHIONABLE BUT SLIGHTLY SORDID ISLINGTON

3 A STERN VICTORIAN EXTERIOR MASKS the fin-de-siècle delights…

DERELICT DOSS HOUSE

AN AIR OF GENTEEL DECAY

UPPER CLASS DOCTOR PROUDLY OFFERS HIS SCRUFFIEST & GRUBBIEST COTTAGE IN BEST OXFORDSHIRE VILLAGE

Don't be misled by the exterior, it's worse inside.

…in the seedier part of the royal Boro of Kensington.

…exposed to the ravages of 5 children.

Decorative defects include a fine growth of fungus on wall of ground-flr rear room.

Do not risk British humor on Americans. Even Roy Brooks got criticized on occasion by his fellow Brits.

When "Negs" Do Work on Americans

Americans will, however, respond exceedingly well to negativism in real estate advertising when it refers to distressed property. There are many serious buyers searching classified for run-down real estate:

1. Builders
2. Entrepreneurs
3. Bargain Mongers
4. Artists
5. Weekend Warriors

1. People in the **building trades** have the skills to replumb, rewire, reroof, paint, set tile. They buy distressed properties, fix them up for resale, or live in them. Building contractors and developers sometimes buy really gross houses for lot value, tear down the structure, and build something new.

2. **Entrepreneurs** have market know-how. They know style. They are good managers. They fix up lousy properties for resale. One of the best known of such entrepreneurs is Suzanne Brangham, author of *Housewise.*

3. **Bargain mongers** are those to whom buying anything retail is an insult to their manhood. They are sure they can beat the system. They buy distressed properties, convinced that they can get them into pristine condition cheaper than the pros, often by hiring moonlighters and illegal immigrants. Bargain mongers usually end up frustrated. The job takes three times as long to complete as anticipated. The work costs three times as much as they figured. Their marriages suffer.

4. **Artists,** by profession or in spirit, are those to whom the process of fix-up is an art form. They are inspired to turn a sow's ear into a silken purse. To them, a dump is a vacant canvas upon which they will paint with their own individual style.

5. **Weekend warriors** are kids who can't afford to live in the area of their choice unless they buy a house in poor condition. They have enough youthful energy, stamina, and drive to increase value with their "sweat equity."

"Never is heard a disparaging word" except when seeking out such fixer-upper folks:

YUK!

3

DEFERRED MAINTENANCE

HANDYMAN SPECIAL

RENTERS' RUIN

WANTED: ELBOW GREASE

BRING MOP, PAINTBRUSH, SHOVEL

GRUNGE LOOK

DIRTY BUT CHEAP

EL DUMPO

"EL DUMPO" and "DIRTY BUT CHEAP" were two of the most successful classified real estate ads ever published in the West.

While such disparaging ads attract buyers, they will lose listings when they insult the sellers. Disparaging ads will offend owners in residence. They will offend heirs who are sentimental about the property or their benefactors who lived in them. Investors won't mind. Banks that have foreclosed won't mind. Relocation companies that inventory real estate won't mind. Sometimes really desperate homeowners won't mind. When in doubt, pass it by the sellers of the property before the copy goes to press.

Advertising Rentals

The same copywriting guidelines apply when advertising rentals. However, advertising residential rental property is a real budget breaker. Realty companies often find that they lose money when they subtract advertising, as well as other expenses, from net commission.

Some firms will not advertise a rental unless the landlord is a valued repeat client. Some bite the bullet and accept the loss in order to promote the firm as being one that offers "full-service residential brokerage."

Recommendation: Take an up-front nonrefundable fee for advertising on all rental listings under a certain price.

Recommendation: Brief all the company rentals in a single weekly one-column ad.

Recommendation: Publish the epitome of vanilla ads:

RENTALS
Apartments from $300.
Houses from $600.

Advertising Vacant Land

Vacant land—city lots, suburban lots, unimproved country property—often takes four times as long to sell as improved property. So the recommended rule of thumb, advertise each property four times a month, does not apply. Giving much advertising to vacant land listings could gobble up commissions. Advertising vacant land once a month is more than ample:

DOWNTOWN LOT

LAKEFRONT LOTS

WINE COUNTRY ACREAGE

WITH FIVE RODS ON GREEN RIVER

ZONED R 4

3

Advertise certain features pertinent to land:

VIEW! VIEW! VIEW!

BARLEY CROP PLANTED

PHEASANT & GROUSE

FARMLAND NEAR PACKING PLANT

UTILITIES IN

TOPOS IN OFFICE

PLANS IN OFFICE

WILL BUILD TO SUIT

"PLANS IN OFFICE" and "WILL BUILD TO SUIT" offer choices to buyers on the cusp. These are buyers who can go either way. They call in on unimproved property ads, but sometimes end up buying ready-made houses that fit their want list.

Ads for Investment Properties

Residential investment properties are advertised as often as owner-occupied dwellings.

Some pertinent investment-type language is included in the ads:

FINANCIALS IN OFFICE

ONE PERCENT VACANCY

FULLY OCCUPIED

RECENTLY RENOVATED

ON-SITE MANAGER

10% CAP RATE

Goodwill

Classified advertising can be used to promote **goodwill** for a realty company. Make friends:

PROUD OF OUR POLICE FORCE

CONGRATS! SEQUOIA HI FOOTBALL TEAM

Designed by master architect ROBERT BLUNK

BUY OUR ENGLISH TUDOR
Celebrate at Agatha's English Tea Room

Tooting Your Own Horn

Classified advertising can be used to send positive messages about a realty firm:

WE SPEAK 7 LANGUAGES:
French
Spanish
Italian
Cantonese
Japanese
Swedish
German

3

MANSION MERCHANTS

PURVEYOR OF PRESTIGE HOMES

FACILITATORS FOR FIRST-TIME BUYERS

ESTABLISHED IN 1976

ALL FULL-TIME AGENTS

RELOCATION SPECIALISTS
1,500 broker network

WE DON'T WASH WINDOWS,
BUT WE DO WORK HOLIDAYS

Entice Readers with Giveaways

Everyone likes to receive gifts. When you offer giveaways, readers not only will respond to ads, but also may provide your realty company with their names and addresses:

SEND FOR COPY OF NEW SEWER LATERAL LAW

HAVE SCHOOL SCHEDULE, WILL MAIL

COME IN FOR YOUR FREE MAP

CALL FOR TROJANS GAME SCHEDULE

CALL FOR FACT SHEETS

CARE FOR A BROCHURE?

Churning Them Out

Churning out dynamite ad copy month in and month out is a challenge. Your favorite words and ideas can become stale, like ten-month-old listings. Copywriters need to find ways to recharge their batteries, ways to gather new words and new ideas for use in the pursuit of public attention.

Read and Listen

Develop a copywriter's third eye and third ear. See and hear more clearly than mortal beings. Collect words and ideas in your writer's database or in a shoe box.

Recommendation: Read a newspaper every day. Read magazines. Read junk mail. Keep the radio tuned on to the news station all day, in the automobile, in the kitchen, in the john. Listen to real estate agents talk. Listen to civilians talk.

> *Life is our dictionary.*
>
> —Ralph Waldo Emerson

Recommendation: Get yourself a shoe box in which to store your collectibles. Collect notes. Collect bits and pieces from the newspaper, magazines, and junk mail. Have your roomy clip for you from his newspaper, magazines, and junk mail.

Recommendation: Keep yourself immune to plain vanilla advertising. Do not read classified real estate advertising more than once a year. Else you could become infected with the dread vanilla ooze, that debilitating disease that has afflicted those writers of bland copy.

When you do read classified real estate advertising, every year or so, read it with purpose. Do your competitors' ads stand out? Why do they stand out?

Recommendation: Draw up a list of all the words the other advertisers are using too many times. They may be:

Immaculate
Spacious
Beautiful
Charming
Rancher
Offered at
Asking price

"Offered at" and "Asking price" suggest to readers that the printed price is subject to low offers. As a seller, this would bother me.

Get yourself an elastic band. Put it around your wrist. Every time you type one of those overused words, snap it. Then press the delete button and open up your thesaurus.

You're Great to Have Around, Kid

Classified real estate copywriters are interesting people. They are aware. They can express themselves in a few well-chosen words. They make stimulating dinner partners and delightful, with-it grandparents.

To Agents

Squeeze every last bit of value out of your dynamite classified advertising.

Take copies of your ads with you when you go on a listing presentation. Show is better than "Tell you what I'm going to do for you, Mr. Seller."

If you can find a tear sheet where your company's ad stands out amongst all the others, take that along too.

Use classified to keep your seller satisfied with your marketing efforts. Paste each ad on a piece of stationery and send it to your seller the day it comes out in the newspaper. Put down the date it was published and in which newspaper. (If the ad is a wee three liner, note the circulation of the paper. A hundred thousand subscribers will justify "wee.") Include comments with the ad copy: "Got ten calls on this one!" "Don't your suggestions look swell in print?"

Proselytize with your dynamite ad copy. Staple together, with your business card, copies of the published ads on your listing. After the sellers move out, leave it on a shelf where the new owners will find it one day. You will be the agent they remember when they go to sell the property in the future.

Roy Brooks Estate Agents prints postcards of Roy Brooks's outrageous advertisements. What a smart farming tool! How about doing that with your ads?

Wear a Bullet-Proof Vest

4

Copywriters need to protect themselves and their realty companies against enemies by being responsible authors.

The public is always ready to criticize the real estate profession. Nationally 70 percent of those who have dealt with Realtors are satisfied with their agents' performance. That's an admirable figure when one considers the complexities of the job. On the other hand, less than 20 percent of the public at large trusts real estate agents in general. Irresponsible advertising fuels that public mistrust.

The legal profession makes a lot of money from the real estate profession. Watch out. Lawyers have used classified real estate ads as evidence of misrepresentation and fraud in their lawsuits. There is nothing so frightening to a manager or a real estate agent as receiving a subpoena.

Write with a picayune buyer, your critical public and competitors, and F. Lee Bailey, Esq., looking over your shoulder.

4 Enthuse Plenty, But Don't Exaggerate Plenty

A view is not AWESOME if it can be seen only from a closet window.

A view is not INSPIRING if it overlooks the recycling plant.

A kitchen is not THE ULTIMATE in convenience if it lacks a compactor.

The decor is not STYLISH if it is stained.

A mansion is not MAGNIFICENT if it is badly in need of paint.

In "Read Between Lines of Real Estate Ads," Mark Patinkin, of the *Providence* (Rhode Island) *Journal,* writes:

Homeowners, I've found, have a strange habit. Even when we're not in the market for a new house, we tend to spend Sunday mornings perusing the real estate section. I'm not sure why we do it, except maybe to assure ourselves that we got a good deal.

The more I peruse, the more I see that real estate agents write ads in code. I thought I'd tell you what the ads really say:

"Cozy"— Miniature.

"Adorable"— Infinitesimal.

"The Perfect First-Time Investment"— You won't want to stay in this dump any longer than you have to.

"Like New"—Decorated this decade.

"Gracious Entry Hall"—Two people can fit in it.

"Price Reduced"—From $298,000 to $297,500.

"Possible Second-Story Water View"—Depends on how powerful the binoculars are.

"Antique"—The wiring is from the 18th century.

"In-Law Apartment"—A hot plate in the basement.

"Charming"—Hasn't been painted since the '20s.

"Bring Your Bathing Suit"—Plastic pool in back yard.

"Almost Two-Acre Lot"—1.1 acres.

"Direct Access to Shopping"—Located over a gas station.

"Sale by Owner"—If this guy's so cheap he doesn't want to pay an agent's commission, you should see the corners he's cut on the house.

"Super Starter"—One small bedroom.

"Expandable"—Not even one small bedroom.

"Owner Motivated"—Has been trying to unload this shack for 18 months.

"Seconds to freeway"—The roar of 18-wheelers will lull you to sleep each night.

"Twelve-Minute Commute to Central City"—At 2 A.M.

"Wood-Burning Stove"—In lieu of furnace.

"Original Detail"—Same paint job as when built in 1910.

"Casual"—Doors falling off hinges.

"The Setting Alone Is Worth the Price"—The house certainly isn't.

"Nestled Among Fine Homes"—The dog of the block.

"Priced to sell"—Owner has gone bankrupt and is hoping a phrase like this will convince you it's a giveaway.

"Open Floor Plan"—No inside walls.

"Partially Unfinished"—No outside walls.

"Handyman's special"—How do you feel about installing a new roof?

"Needs TLC"—May the Lord help you.

Present a True Picture

The *Code of Ethics and Standards of Practice* of the National Association of Realtors states:

Realtors shall be careful at all times to present a true picture in their advertising and representations to the public.

—Article 19

The loveliest fourth bedroom is not to be considered a true fourth bedroom if can be entered only through another bedroom or bath-room.

A basement playroom is not a true playroom if the ceiling height does not meet code standards.

A garage converted into a family room is still a garage so long as there remains the slightest hint that it was originally built to house a vehicle.

A pool site is not an acceptable pool site if a swimming pool cannot be constructed under normal conditions.

We once sold a ranch-style house to a charming couple from England. **POOL SITE** in our ad was what attracted them. Pool construction began the day the English couple moved in. The bulldozer unearthed a huge granite boulder four feet under the surface. Since zoning disallowed dynamite, the boulder had to be jackhammered out bit by bit by a single laborer. The pool took three times as long to build as estimated. It cost three times as much money. Fortunately for us, the couple did not sue. In England *caveat emptor* (buyer beware) still prevails. Fortunately for the English couple, when they were transferred again five years later, the house sold for twice what they had paid for it.

Another broker in town was not so fortunate with his "pool site." He had to pay to have the main sewer line relocated.

Do Not Quote Measurements

Some prospects are annoyed that we cautious Realtors are reluctant to quote measurements. It is for good reason. Even though dimensions quoted in ads may be taken from the best authorities, they can be inaccurate. It is the realty company that is held accountable, no matter what authority provided them.

The tax records often err. Building plans often do not reflect changes made after construction has commenced. Lot descriptions in prelims are hard to read. Figuring the dimensions of irregular lots requires a pile of math.

So don't risk printing erroneous information by quoting dimensions in classified. Your agents can promise to lend ad callers their five-hundred-foot measuring tapes later on.

A realty company made the mistake of giving lot measurements, which had been copied from an old multiple listing book, in a classified home ad. A nice man bought the home. Afterward, it was discovered that one dimension was shy thirty inches. The nice man lost his job, turned sour, and sued the realty company that sold him the property. The ad was his lawyer's primary evidence. The realty company settled by buying the home, paying the legal fees, and compensating the man for emotional distress.

There may be times when lot size or acreage is information crucial to an ad. In that case, give approximations and/or figures below those printed in the records:

Lot About One Acre
(According to the *Realdex,* it is over an acre)

Over Six Acres
(The map book shows it to be 6½)

There's Danger in Them Thar Words

It seems that the attorneys who specialize in protecting the real estate industry would be happier if we agents published only plain vanilla ads. Certain words make them cringe. For instance, they advise us never, never to use the words guaranty, excellent, perfect, expert, or best.

Hugh F. Connolly, legal counsel for two California realty boards, former member of the California Association of Realtors legal task force, and protector of the realty profession for over thirty years, warns:

A real estate agent is in no position to warrant the quality or quantity of property the agent is marketing—the law doesn't require it, and no one should be led to expect it.

4

Therefore, agents should avoid using words in advertising that suggest a representation or warrant of quality or quantity.

For example, compare: "Pool site available" with "Buyers should ask about pool site."

The first is a warranty, the second is not. But the second will equally catch the eye of a buyer interested in a possible pool.

Compare: "House in excellent condition" with "If you're choosy, see this house."

Compare: "1.5 acre lot" with "Bring some help to measure this lot!"

Compare: "Brand new roof" with "Ask about roof warranty."

Compare: "Perfect" with "Gorgeous."

Compare: "Five thousand square foot house" with "You Want Big? See This One!"

More Never-Nevers

Safe and Secure: The public is particularly interested these days in living in a safe and secure environment. Good ad copy may address that interest without promising that a property is absolutely "safe" or "secure." "Safety Features" and "Security System" give the message without making the listing office subject to suit should a future buyer trip over a loose brick or be ripped off on the premises.

All: This little word can be a real bugaboo when used without due caution. For instance, "All Electric Kitchen," or AEK, is inaccurate if the kitchen has a gas-fired barbecue. "All Copper Pipes," when referring to an older home, is risky. The owner may tell his agent that the house has been all replumbed with copper pipe. He may have the bills to prove it. Then someone finds a section of galvanized pipe embedded in a wall. Check it out: Is the property actually "All reroofed," or did the roofer skip the potting shed?

Free: This is a word known to attract positive attention in advertising, yet it can also attract trouble. No access that accommodates vehicles is totally "traffic free." The day your "noise-free neighborhood" ad comes out in print, a neighbor takes up the clarinet. Or the worst windstorm in recorded history hits the week your "wind-free" ad is published. "Free" used in such a context means without-any-of-it. Substitute: "Low traffic," "Serene," "Sheltered."

Est: Tacking "est" onto the back of words can be complaint bait. Can you prove that your listing is the "'newest," the "oldest," the "biggest," or the "cheapest"?

Abide by the Golden Rule

The National Association of Realtors addresses the obligation of all its members to cooperate with one another:

> *Whatsoever ye would that others should do to you, do ye even so to them.*
> —*Code of Ethics and Standards of Practice,* Preamble

> *Realtors shall cooperate with other brokers except when cooperation is not in the client's best interest.*
> —Article 22

Printing "Principals Only" in a classified ad tells agents in other offices that the listing company denies their participation in the selling of the property. In other words, "We are not cooperating." This is bad policy. While brokers would prefer to sell their listings in-house and thus retain the entire commission, blatantly announcing lack of cooperation kills friendship with the peers who may be needed to help sell other company listings. (Some Realtors who do "principals only" advertising say they are justified in doing so where the listings are not being processed through the Board of Realtors Multiple Listing Service. Who do they think they're kidding? The *Code of Ethics,* Article 22, clearly addresses its membership in the matter of cooperation, without exclusion. It is not addressing classification of listings.)

4

Printing "New Listing" or "Just Listed" in an ad, in order to make the phones ring about a property that has been in the company inventory for months, is not an uncommon marketing tool. It is a dishonest one. Such tactics will not go unnoticed by competitors. The competitors have every right to take potshots at realty companies who use them. Those companies deserve to be censured by the Ethics Committee of the Board of Realtors.

Proof, Proof, Proof

Proof your work. Double-check your descriptive words, the price, the number of bedrooms, the number of bathrooms, the addresses in the open home ads. Be careful not to call a "lane" a "street." Sellers get ticked off at that one.

Reproof old ads that you are rerunning. You don't want to leave in that "new listing" language by mistake.

After you have proofed your ads, before they go to the newspaper, deliver copies to the listing agents for them to proof. Deliver the ad copy to your manager for him to proof, even if you have to follow him home.

Proofing Is the Guardian Angel of Copywriters!

Be Ready to Eat Crow

No matter how hard a creative copywriter tries to please, no matter how diligently the copy is proofed, it will eventually offend someone. And when it offends, the copywriter, the manager, and the agents eat crow. They apologize until they're blue in the face in order to protect the company's good name and keep the legal enemies from the door.

We listed a very special Spanish-style home. At the time there was a new subdivision in town where the homes were being marketed as

"Spanish." The only "Spanish" apparent in those spec houses was the terra-cotta paint and the vinyl floors designed to look somewhat like Spanish tiles. Our special Spanish home had imported clay tiles, wrought-iron work, hand-stenciled beams, rough-hewn floors. I thought up a dandy headline to indicate authenticity of our listing: "NO TACO BELL." A call came into the office from the furious franchise owner of a local Taco Bell take-out restaurant. Our ad had insulted her place of business. The floor person who took the call apologized. She handed the phone to me. I apologized. We sent the owner a letter of apology. I ordered burritos for everyone in the office. We yanked the ad, which was scheduled to run again. We also scratched "NO COLONEL SANDERS" from our Georgian colonial ad.

Check and double-check your sources if your information is not in writing.

We listed a house owned by a gourmet cook. She bemoaned the fact that she was leaving the neighborhood just as a renowned gourmet market was moving in. That provocative bit of information was printed in our ad. The ad brought us a letter from an attorney threatening to sue on behalf of the owner of the existing neighborhood market, who said our ad had driven away customers. This attorney was no small potatoes in our town. We were terrified. As head of the company, I wrote a letter to the attorney and had it hand delivered the same day. In the letter I assured him that the offending ad would never run again; and I asked him, please, to make our sincere apologies to his client. As it turned out, we did not get sued. The renowned gourmet market eventually bought the existing market from the owner who had wanted to sue us. While our information was factual, the sale of the market was not a done deal at the time the ad went to press. It is assumed that our announcement put a crimp in negotiations. The story has a happy ending. The terrifying attorney bought a million-dollar house from us two years later.

Eating crow fast and graciously sometimes turns enemies into friends.

4 More "Cautionaries"

Cover your flank by writing with fair-housing activists looking over your shoulder.

The Fair Housing Act was enacted in 1968, then amended in 1989. The Department of Housing and Urban Development takes the position that newspapers face civil suits for publication of housing advertisements that violate the Fair Housing Act. These include advertisements that encourage discrimination or even indicate a preference on the grounds of race, color, religion, sex, handicap, familial status, or national origin.

Handicap refers to any physical or mental impairment, including alcoholism. People so afflicted may not be denied housing. (Addiction to illegal use of a controlled substance is excluded from the handicap provision.) On the other hand, advertising may encourage occupancy by handicapped persons.

Familial status refers to persons under eighteen years of age who live with a parent or guardian.

It is permissible to advertise housing for the **elderly**, providing that the housing:

A. is designed and operated to assist **older** persons under a government program
B. is to be occupied solely by persons over sixty-two
C. has at least 80 percent of its units occupied by at least one person over fifty-five.

(Retirement communities qualify as housing for elderly persons.)

Nonprofit housing provided by **religious** organizations may limit occupants to those of the same religion providing that the religious organization does not restrict its membership on the basis of race, color, or national origin.

Housing may reasonably limit the maximum number of occupants. Shared-housing ads may give sex preference.

Other HUD No-No's

Certain **symbols** or **logotypes,** such as a crucifix or the Star of David, that imply race, color, religion, sex, handicap, familial status, or national origin may not be used in advertising.

Colloquialisms, used regionally or locally, that give meaning deemed to be discriminatory are forbidden.

Giving directions indicating in any way that the location is within or outside of an area that is predominantly minority is forbidden. Directions should not use **religious landmarks** as identification (churches, parish buildings, temples).

Naming facilities in directions such as **clubs** and **private schools** that cater to certain religious or ethnic groups is restricted.

Fair-Housing Activists Marched

In 1991, fair-housing activists sued thirteen newspapers in Oregon for lack of compliance. The Oregon Newspaper Publishers Association, representing the newspapers, settled the case by paying the plaintiffs' litigation costs and by agreeing to develop training materials to educate its members. As part of the materials, the Oregon Newspaper Publishers Association drew up a list of words and phrases that it interprets to be acceptable, unacceptable, or questionable. Some newspapers in other states have adopted the Oregon list; others have drawn up their own lists, since different words mean different things to people in different places. Copywriters should get lists from their own newspapers. As an example of what to expect, here is the Oregon list of okay, "never-never," and questionable words and phrases:

Acceptable
Close to downtown
Den

Family room
Generic places
Near
No smoking/drinking
Number of bedrooms
One Apartment
Play area
Privacy
Private setting
School district
Schools
Secluded
Security provided
Senior discount (context by itself)
Seniors (if certified by HUD as senior housing)
Square feet
Townhouse
Tradition (style of home)
View
Walking distance to…

Unacceptable
Adult (adult building, adult park, etc.)
Adults only
Bachelor
Bachelor pad
Black
Blind
Board approval
Catholic church
Christian
Couple (couple preferred, couples only, etc.)
Crippled
Deaf

Drinker(s)
Ethnic landmarks
Executive
Exclusive
Family (great for families)
Female
Gentleman's farm
Grandma's house
Handicap limitations (not suitable for)
Handicapped
Integrated
Jewish
Male
Man
Marital status
Membership approval
Mentally handicapped
Mentally ill
Mentally retarded
Mormon temple
Name of school
Nationality (Oriental, Hispanic, etc.)
No children
No play area
Number of people
Older person, senior citizen
One child
One person
Oriental
Physically fit person (ideal for, limited to)
Private
Race
Religious landmark
Religious name

Restricted

Retired

Senior, senior discount

Sex (except in advertising for roommates)

Single

Single person

Smoker(s)

Student

Traditional (settings)

Two people

White

Woman

Words descriptive of dwelling landlord and tenants

Questionable

Executive

Female roommate

55 and older (must meet HUD guidelines)

Male roommate

Neighborhood

Older persons

Some of Oregon's words and phrases go without saying; others you may think goofy. Your newspaper will probably not be nearly so strict with its list of "never-never" words and phrases. Understandably, the Oregonians got spooked.

California Newspaper Publishers' Association Speaks

The California Newspaper Publishers' Association (CNPA) says:

Remember, Describe the Property, Not the People.

The CNPA made up this motto after the Oregon newspapers had their trouble with the fair-housing activists. With all due respect to the exalted CNPA, this motto should be trashed.

As venerable real estate broker Howard Blitz oft said, "It's not the nest. It's the birdies in the nest."

People buy the lifestyle first and the structure second. Mom wants to know that there are playmates for her children in the neighborhood more than she wants to know about stucco siding. Mr. Chairman-of-the-Board likes proximity to fine dining and suitable clubs more than he likes laundry rooms and double sinks. Single women are more attracted by buildings where single guys live than they are to buildings that have won architectural awards. Talk to the "birdies":

HARASSED, HARRIET?
STRESSED OUT, SANDRA?
CURSIN' THE COMMUTE, CHARLES?
WE'LL MOVE YOU CLOSER TO WORK

COLLECT ANTIQUES?

FITNESS FREAK?

FOR THOSE SEEKING PEACE & QUIET

Mr. Roy Brooks, in the *London Sunday Times* and *Observer*, addressed the birdies in most of his funky classified ads:

HER HIGHNESS GEORGINA
THE MAHARANEE OF COOCH BEHAR

REVOLUTIONARY PIANO TEACHER MUST SELL

LABOUR SAVING CASTLE: The lucky buyer of this erection...

4 IF YOU WISH TO LIVE DECENTLY behind the modest and unobjectionable facade of an early Victorian house in which the remnants of Georgian good taste linger...

HAIRY ARCHITECT'S DRAMATIC Ent flr Mais

DESPERATE ENGLISHMAN & FRENCH GIRL would consider anything sordid

IF YOU ARE PREPARED TO LIVE in one of the more backward urban areas where they still only empty your dustbin once a week...

Will only sell for single occupancy to gentle people

HUNGARIAN RETURNING TO IBIZA with Gentlewoman

LITTLE VENICE. Not only fashionable but, judging by the neighbours, a veritable compost heap of culture.

ERSTWHILE MAKER OF SECRET WEAPONS TAKING UP DRINK, Forced sacrifice...

YOUNG MRS. DOUCH THE DOCTOR'S WIFE ("I'm frequently taken for the au pair girl.") enthusiastically recommends her cheerful, superbly modernized Victorian Ealing Family House to anyone like herself with 5 children under 6½.

Fair-Housing Statement

Several times each year add some fair-housing language to your classified advertising. "Committed to Fair Housing and Equal Opportunity Employment," or "We shall not deny equal professional services to any person for reasons of race, color, religion, sex, handicap, familial status, or national origin. We shall not be a party to any plan or agreement to discriminate against a person or persons on the basis of race, color, religion, sex, handicap, familial status, or national origin." Should your company ever be accused of discrimination, this public statement will give proof of intent.

Reg Z and Advertising

Cover your flank. Write with the Federal Reserve Board looking over your shoulder.

The Truth and Lending Act, Regulation Z, was enacted by the Federal Reserve Board in 1969, modified in 1984, to help consumers of real estate understand credit terms prior to entering into binding transactions. Real estate professionals are required to comply with certain conditions when advertising one to two residential properties in the following categories:

Attached Single-Family Houses
Two Detached Units on One Lot or Parcel
Condominiums
Cooperative Units
Townhouses
Duplexes
Farms & Ranches with Residences
Mobile Homes

Reg Z applies only where specific numbers (those problematic numbers again), specific words, specific phrases are used. For example:

7% Fixed Rate
30-Year Fixed Rate

4

4% Variable
$1,000 PITI
Points 2%
$4,000 Down Payment

When the interest rate is given, advertising must include the Annual Percentage Rate, APR. Points have to be stated in dollar amounts and as an annual percentage rate if paid in installments. Any anticipated rate increase after consummation must be stated. The period of the loan must be stated.

Some Quotes from Reg Z

1662. Advertising of downpayments and installments.
No advertisement to aid, promote, or assist directly or indirectly any extension of consumer credit may state
    (1) that a specific periodic consumer credit amount or installment amount can be arranged, unless the creditor usually and customarily arranges credit payments or installments for that period and in that amount.
    (2) that a specified downpayment is required in connection with any extension of consumer credit, unless the creditor usually and customarily arranges down payments in that amount.
1663. Advertising of open end credit plans.
No advertisement to aid, promote, or assist directly or indirectly the extension of consumer credit under an open end credit plan may set forth any of the specific terms of that plan unless it also clearly and conspicuously sets forth all of the following items:
    (1) Any minimum for fixed amount which could be imposed.
    (2) In any case in which periodic rates may be used to compute the finance charge, the periodic rates expressed as annual percentage rates.
    (3) Any other term that the Board may by regulation require to be disclosed.
1664. Advertising of credit other than open end plans.
Exclusion of open end credit plans
(a) Except as provided in subsection (b) of this section, this section applies to any advertisement to aid, promote, or assist directly or indirectly any consumer credit sale, loan, or other extension of credit subject to the provisions of this subchapter, other than an open end credit plan.
Advertisements of residential real estate
(b) The provisions of this section do not apply to advertisements or residential real estate except to the extent that the Board may by regulation require.
Rate of finance charge expressed as annual percentage rate
(c) If any advertisement to which this section applies states the rate of a finance charge, the advertisement shall state the rate of that charge expressed as an annual percentage rate.
Requisite disclosures in advertisement
(d) If any advertisement to which this section applies states the amount of the downpayment, if any, the amount of any installment payment, the dollar amount of any finance charge, or the number of installments or the period of repayment, then the advertisement shall state all of the following items:
    (1) The downpayment, if any.
    (2) The terms of repayment.
    (3) The rate of the finance charge expressed as an annual percentage rate.
226.16 Advertising
(a) **Actually available terms.** If an advertisement for credit states specific credit terms, it shall state only those terms that actually are or will be arranged or offered by the creditor.

(b) **Advertisement of terms that require additional disclosures.** If any of the terms required to be disclosed under 226.6 is set forth in an advertisement, the advertisement shall also clearly and conspicuously set forth the following:

(1) Any minimum, fixed, transaction, activity or similar charge that could be imposed.

(2) Any periodic rate that may be applied expressed as an annual percentage rate as determined under 226.14(b). If the plan provides for a variable periodic rate that too shall be disclosed.

(3) Any membership or participation fee that could be imposed.

226.24 Advertising

(a) **Actually available terms.** If an advertisement for credit states specific credit terms, it shall state only those terms that actually are or will be arranged offered by the creditor.

(b) **Advertisement of rate of finance charge.** If an advertisement states a rate of finance charge, it shall state the rate as an "annual percentage rate," using that term. If the annual percentage rate may be increased after consummation, the advertisement shall state that fact.

The advertisement shall not state any other rate, except that a simple annual rate or periodic rate that is applied to an unpaid balance may be stated in conjunction with, but not more conspicuously than, the annual percentage rate.

(c) **Advertisement of terms that require additional disclosures.** (1) If any of the following terms is set forth in an advertisement, the advertisement shall meet the requirements of paragraph (c)(2) of this section:

(i) The amount or percentage of any downpayment.

(ii) The number of payments or period of repayment.

(iii)The amount of any payment.

(iv) The amount of any finance charge.

(2) An advertisement stating any of the terms in paragraph (c)(1) of this section shall state the following, as applicable:

(i) The amount or percentage of the downpayment.

(ii) The terms of repayment.

(iii)The annual percentage rate, using that term, and, if the rate may be increased after consummation, that fact.

—*United States Code Annotated,* Title 15

Recommendation: Reg Z applies to any financing offered by any lender other than the owner. When advertising financing offered by any lender, including the owner, it is a smart idea to have the commitment documented, signed, and on file in the real estate office.

Recommendation: Though Reg Z does not advise this, it is wise to cover all bases by adding the following language, where it applies, when quoting loan terms:

<u>Some</u> 6% Loans Available

To Qualified Buyers

Will Consider

May Lend

Without such cautionary language, some buyers, new to the real estate game, might get the wrong notion that the stated lending terms are offered to everyone, unconditionally, without the usual requirements for personal financial qualification.

Classified ads that provide all the credit data required by Reg Z, usually expensive Sunday display ads, most often feature multiple units such as new housing tracts and condominium buildings. The developer, or his institutional lender, is offering an advantageous loan package as an inducement to purchase.

Credit Terms Don't Make Dynamite Copy

A lot of credit language does little to entice the average classified reader, unless the loan terms are incredibly good, like having an interest rate 3 percent below the going rate. Few readers analyze classified with their calculators.

You can get just as much mileage, and bypass the Feds, by briefly indicating that good terms are available. (Let the sales agents discuss financial details. Better still, let the sales agents put the prospective buyers your enticing ads have attracted in touch with the lender.) For example:

GOOD TERMS

Lender offers special finance terms

LOW DOWN PAYMENT

Interesting Interest Rate

Owner Financing Available

ASSUMABLE LOAN

BIG Assumable Loan

Try FHA

Try VA

ASK ABOUT OUR NICE LOAN DEAL

Do Not Be Intimidated by the Limitations

You can write your dynamite ads and still protect the company and yourself. Simply omit words and phrases that guarantee, overexaggerate, are inaccurate, or could be perceived as discriminatory. You've got 150,000 entries in *Webster's New World Dictionary* from which to choose.

"Orson [Welles] said to me at lunch one day that the enemy of art is the absence of limitations," said movie director Henry Jaglom (*Eating*). In fact, limitation could be your mother of creativity as it has been for others:

Alicia Markova, one of the century's greatest prima ballerinas, was originally sent to ballet school to strengthen muscles weakened by polio.

Swimmer Ann Curtis won a gold medal in the 1948 Olympic Games. Her road to success began when she was seven years old. That year, Ann and her sister, Sue, spent a lonely summer in a convent in Santa Rosa, California. There were no other children to play with. There were no activities provided. But there was a swimming pool!

Dr. Seuss wrote and illustrated wonderful children's books (*Cat in the Hat, Green Eggs and Ham, Horton Hatches the Egg,* etc.). His bizarre, funny fantasy animal characters are loved by children around the world. Dr. Seuss once explained that he drew bizarre, funny fantasy animals for his books because he didn't have the skill to draw realistic ones.

My artist mother created one of her most striking still-life paintings after little Joanie had snacked on the fruit.

To Agents

We real estate professionals have been well schooled in the use of cautionary language: to be accurate in our reporting, to check our figures, and not to mislead the public.

Residential real estate professionals are committed to fair-housing practices. Our profession is probably the most self-patrolled of all on anti-discrimination.

Nevertheless, it might be useful for you to review this chapter from time to time. It might also be useful for you to make a copy of some of the HUD fair-housing directives to have on hand should a seller ask you to advertise for a certain type of buyer: "I don't want to sell to foreigners." "Find me a family just like ours."

Make it a habit to proof the ads on every one of your listings, no matter who writes them. Don't be afraid to correct others' mistakes, even if the copywriter is your boss. Don't be afraid to request changes. You know your listings and the sensitivities of your sellers better than anybody.

My Buddy, My Newspaper

Newspapers are poised, ready to serve their customers. But unless realty companies establish close working relationships with their newspapers, the most dynamite ad copy may not appear dynamite in print. While classified personnel are trained and skilled in reproducing copy, they cannot be expected to do their best if realty companies do not communicate their objectives, and if they do not deliver clear copy with adequate directions in a timely fashion. At the outset of every classified campaign, real estate management and classified personnel should get together for a good-buddy rap session.

Before making an appointment to get together, a realty manager has to choose the right good buddy. It is very important to choose the newspaper that will serve your real estate company best in your marketplace. You may have many newspapers to choose from:

1. **Local Dailies**
2. **Local Weeklies**
3. **Metropolitan Giant**

4. Ethnic Newspapers
5. Trade and Special-Interest Papers
6. Out-of-Area Newspapers

1. In every area it is the **daily newspaper** that offers realty firms the most mileage. It may be a morning newspaper or an evening newspaper.

2. **Weeklies** that service the realty firm's primary target area are effective. While their circulation may be only 5,000 readers, they may be well read by the townies who love articles about the high school basketball team, Boy Scout activities, and their neighbors' accomplishments.

3. **Metropolitan** newspapers with wide coverage reach suburban towns and rural communities as well as their home-base cities.

4. The explosion of immigration to the United States has caused a proliferation of **ethnic newspapers,** printed in foreign languages.

Sellers might request advertising in ethnic newspapers. While merchants speak of good sales from ethnic newspapers, purchasing real estate is a hundred times more complex than purchasing sofas and shoes. Don't waste your money advertising in an ethnic, unless you have several licensees in the office who speak the language and can handle all calls that result. (Imagine being attracted by an ad featuring a vacation home on the Amazon River. When you call in, no one in the realty office speaks anything but tribal Yanamano.) Besides, unless you have someone who can translate, you will never know if your ad came out in the ethnic paper the way you wrote it. "Garage" could have been turned into "Garbage."

5. **Trade and other special-interest newspapers** feed the interests of different tradesfolk such as building contractors, medical providers, and accountants. Desktop publishing has made it possible for special-interest groups to publish their own newspapers on a shoestring, feeding the interests of less affluent readers, such as students, religious organizations, and the homeless.

Trade papers and other special-interest newspapers have limited classified sections, if any. Even the people for whom those newspapers are written will not look for real estate there.

Advertising in papers of specialized coverage is not cost-effective unless to do so is the only way to secure a valuable listing. Sellers may demand ads in the *Wall Street Journal*. It is one of the most respected newspapers in the world, but has very limited success as an advertiser of residential real estate. Instead of advertising in the *Journal*, keep a copy in your reception area. The *Journal* will add more class to the place than a four-foot philodendron.

Realty firms should choose newspapers in which to advertise based first on numbers, not on character or personality. Classified is not the place for pioneering. The best newspaper is the one that publishes the most real estate ads in any realty firm's marketplace. This is where the public is conditioned to look for real estate.

6. Springing for ads in out-of-town newspapers is a waste of money. People looking for housing in your town will logically look for it in your local newspaper. They can send for the local paper, or they may find it in their libraries or at one of those upscale newsstands.

Springing for ads in a newspaper published in a foreign country is a bigger waste of money. People living in foreign countries who plan to purchase property in the United States will make contact with a U.S. broker through business connections or through friends who live here.

JM Tayler & Company Realtors did use "foreign" in a different way on occasion with success. Friends in France and Spain gave us permission to advertise their properties in our local newspaper. The ads did not pull business, even calls, but they sure made us look important!

5

Recommendation: The ideal advertising situation, if your office is outside a big city, is to place ads in a local daily, a local weekly, and a big metropolitan newspaper that serves many zones or regions. At least advertise open homes in the met paper on weekends.

Set the Budget

After you have chosen your buddies, and before your meeting takes place, establish your classified advertising budget.

There are a couple of ways to do so. Do not allot a dollar figure for advertising each listing, or you will be miserable when a cheapie house hangs around for six months eating up the commission as well as the advertising allotment. Of course, you could become ecstatic when a luxury listing sells after being advertised only once. Sometimes, lingering listings attract buyers for other listings. Sometimes sellers demand more advertising than the assigned budget allotment. The allotment method of budgeting is a bookkeeper's nightmare.

Some managers assign a fixed monthly budget, the same for every month of the year, regardless of the number of listings, projected sales prices, or market conditions. Since the inventory and the market climate change from month to month, this method is restrictive. Advertising expenditure should be higher some months than others. When there is a glut of good listings on the market, the budget should be expanded to accommodate more and bigger ads because there is more and bigger competition. When there is a lack of good listings on the open market, the advertising budget can be cut way back. The ads can be little fellows because buyers hunt the newspapers harder then.

The best budget is one established on a yearly basis. A good benchmark is 15 percent of annual overhead. In a location where the use of Multiple Listing Service is all-encompassing, the budget may be lowered. Where only 50 percent of a real estate company's inventory is processed through MLS, the budget should be over 15 percent. The yearly budget should be given monthly flexibility to reflect changes in the number of listings, projected sales prices, and market conditions.

Fit the Budget to the Cost

Before your meeting with the newspaper, get a copy of the newspaper's rate sheet. Check it over so that you have some feeling for the kind of exposure your budget can accommodate.

5

Meet with Your Classified Editor

Arrange a meeting with the classified editor and the representative who will be assigned to your account. Bring along your copywriter, if you have one.

This meeting is worth more advance preparation. You can, in one well-programmed session, establish a fine working relationship with your newspaper, your new best friend. Once the newspaper understands your objectives and once your office is informed as to the proper systems for communicating with the newspaper, the job is done, maybe for years to come.

You will have jotted down items for discussion:

1. **Your Objectives**
2. **Your Budget**
3. **Sizes and Placement of Ads**
4. **Display Ads**
5. **Form in Which Copy Is Submitted**
6. **Schedules**
7. **Billing Procedures**
8. **Your Contact at Newspaper**
9. **Contact at Realty Company**
10. **Newspaper Services and Specials**

1. You will explain, at the meeting, that you intend to make maximum use of classified as your primary source of new business. You will identify **your objectives**. Explain that you expect your classified advertising to attract buyers, sellers, and new sales agents. You intend that classified will present your company as an honorable, professional company, and a company with flair. You will tell the buddies that you seek a large loyal readership that follows your ads for fun and information, a readership that will quote your clever ads around the community. The classified editor will very pleased to know that you are determined to grace his pages with a quality product.

2. Present **your budget** as a range. You may not want to spend your entire budget on one newspaper. Ask for suggestions about how to achieve your goals for maximum exposure while maintaining your budget. Ask the editor to explain the newspaper's contract, how many lines of copy are required to achieve the best overall rate.

3. With the help of the rate sheet and a classified tear sheet, have the editor show you how ads of a specific **size** will look and what they will cost. What are the placement classifications under which various types of real estate are located in the paper? Ask what days pull the most. Be sure to ask if the newspaper processes classified over TV and computers. If so, will that cost you more?

4. Ask about **display ads**. You will want to print your logo in your open home ads, unless you are advertising in a giant metropolitan newspaper. (Your budget will probably not stand up to the cost of a display ad in a newspaper that has a circulation of 100,000 or more readers.) The art department will help you set up the ad with your logo.

What is the newspaper's policy on photos? Using a photo of a house in a display ad attracts attention. For most offices, photo ads are an unaffordable expense, unless the newspaper provides a section where a collection of very small photos is printed. Very small photos should be photos of light-colored houses with uncomplicated architecture, or else the photos can print up fuzzy. Bigger photo ads are more affordable in the weeklies.

Some creative realty companies, with wholesome budgets, are highlighting their ads with charming drawings of houses. Those ads look wonderful. Ads look a bit gobble-de-goop, however, if photos of houses are mixed in with drawings of houses.

5. Discuss the **form in which copy is to be submitted** to the newspaper. Perhaps the newspaper has a printed form for you to use. In any case, include the following information on every page of copy:

5 At the top of the page, give the name of your realty company, with address, phone number, and fax number. Give the name and telephone number of the contact in your office. Next type the date the ad is to appear in the newspaper. Then identify under which classification the ad is to be placed, either by name or by the newspaper's code number.

Leave several lines of space, then type the actual ad, always double or triple spaced. Include your company name, exactly where you want it to be printed, with the telephone number (bold) and address (unless you are submitting a tiny ad).

At the bottom of the page, separated from the copy, type your instructions to the newspaper: "Stet: *Garçonnière,*" "Stet: *Phalaenopsis.*" (Stet is a proofreader's term meaning don't monkey around with this. Let it stand as is.) There will be times when you want give instructions about a certain size type or all caps or upper- and lowercase letters: "Headline all caps, 14 point." (See page 39 for examples of type sizes.)

6. Get clear about **scheduling**. What are the deadlines for submitting copy? What are the deadlines for last-minute changes or "kill" orders? How are holidays handled?

7. Discuss **billing procedures**. Ask the editor to go over a typical bill with you. They are often difficult to understand.

Ask how credits will be noted on your bill should the newspaper make boo-boos. Will they rerun ads corrected? Will they omit faulty ads from your bill? If you are careful in the way you type up your copy, boo-boos will not occur often.

JM Tayler & Company Realtors suffered its share of newspaper mistakes and typos, though we were very exacting. One of the worst errors was when a new rep put another Realtor's name below our ad. Another time the newspaper left out our open homes ad altogether. The classified editor wrote letters of apology to the sellers. Tayler was spelled with an "o" more than once. New reps changed words into abbreviations and acronyms to save us money, for which we definitely were not grateful. A couple of reps, whose vocabularies were not too sophisticated, changed words: "CHIC FRENCH DECOR" became "CHICK FRENCH DECOR." "ECLECTIC" became "ELEC-TRIC." Of course, there were typo slips: "Pools" was printed "pooos," and a tree was a stately "ellm." I am happy to say that in over 15,000 published Tayler ads never once did a newspaper print the wrong price.

8. You will want to be introduced to **your contact at the newspaper.** (The mayor was our rep at the *Boutique and Villager.*) What are your contact's office hours? You will want to decide whether your contact picks up your weekly ad copy, or whether you will fax it into the newspaper. You will not want to mail it. That's too slow. You will not want to telephone ads in, except in dire emergency. You cannot design dynamite-looking ads over the telephone.

9. The newspaper will want to know who is the **contact in your office;** who has the authority to make decisions; who has the authority to change copy (should they discover that *garçonnière* means "bachelor's pad" in French).

10. Ask what **services and special offers your newspaper provides.** Is there an art department at your disposal? Will the newspaper do printing for you? The *San Mateo Times* designed and printed 500 flyers for us, a collage of its satellite newspapers, which we used in our listing presentations. The *Times* and the *San Francisco Chronicle* and *Examiner* invited us to seminars on classified real estate advertising.

Meat 'n' Potatoes Kinda Guy?

There are those realty managers to whom classified advertising writing is not a viable art form. "Just the facts, Ma'am" is how they intend to advertise. To attract attention with facts-only advertising in the crowded classified page, the use of "Spatial Gymnastics and Power Punctuation" is key.

White space attracts attention, more so than text. Throw your business card on a classified page. Squint your eyes. Notice how the white stands out. Use lots of white space. Give your ads wider margins than normal. Double-space your lines of copy.

Black borders also make ads stand out. On the other hand, black backgrounds with white letters are hard to read in a classified column. I think they look ugly too. Color shouts, but is very expensive. Extra punctuation highlights facts: exclams, question marks, hyphens, and lots of bullets.

Ask the art department what art characters they offer: maybe stars, hearts, clovers, trees, pumpkins, musical notes; certainly oversized bullets, squares, arrows, and plus signs.

Have the art department design a standard jazzy format for your "just the facts" ads using "Spatial Gymnastics and Power Punctuation."

Specials

All newspapers have **specials**. Yours may publish a special Centennial Celebration edition, a Presidents' Day Special, or a yearly Home Edition in which real estate companies can submit display ads at a reduced price.

Real Estate Offices Sell Real Estate, Not People

One specialty ad that newspapers like to promote to realty offices is a display ad collection of mug shots of sales agents. Sorry, buddies, these ads are not worth the newsprint on which they're printed. In the first place, it is a strain for realty offices to collect photos of all the troops. Then the faces end up printed different sizes. Some photos are darker than others. Expressions run the gamut. Altogether these ads look gobble-de-goop and the troops look weird. The only value to

102

these mug shot ads is to amuse children. Mine loved to play the "Rogue's Gallery Game." They'd spread the people ad out on the floor, then take turns poking fun at the adults: "She's a hootchie-koochie dancer," "He's a robber," "Daddy would like this snazzy lady," "This old geezer is wearing a toupee," "Her ponytail's too tight," "He just wet his panties."

If push comes to shove with your office prima donnas, you could publish photo ads of prima donna agents who have won awards or sold up a storm. If you're lucky, the pictures will not look like bounty hunters' posters. Require the individual photographed to pay for her own publicity gimmick. Otherwise, the underachievers will accuse the boss of favoring the overachievers, which he does of course.

Personalize?

Newspapers seem to like personalizing, except where HUD flexes its muscles. Your newspaper may advise you to include names of listing agents in your classified ads. Newspapers say that it is friendly to name real-live people. They suggest that by personalizing, a realty agency will dispel the perception of an impersonal, commission-grabbing business operation. Possibly so. Still, with all due respect to the newspaper buddies, take this advice with a grain of salt because:

A. The listing agent named in the ad is seldom in the office when his ad call comes in.
B. Printing the listing agents' names undermines the up desk.

The up desk is the "service center" where sales agents sit when assigned to answer incoming inquiries. Sales agents are not thrilled about this floor duty. They comply willingly only because, at the up desk, they have the opportunity to pick up new customers who call in. Floor people lose that wonderful opportunity to pick up new customers when ad callers ask for specific agents by name.

Of course, where sales agents write and pay for their own ads, as at RE/MAX Properties, management can hardly forbid them to print their own names.

In rare cases an agent has such prominence that it is the agent's name that draws the most response. By all means, in such cases, use the agent's name.

Mary Lou Cacy has been selling residential real estate in Anchorage, Alaska, for twenty years. She is so well known, so well respected, that her name alone makes the phones ring. Pro that she is, Mary Lou makes sure that her callers receive fast attention. She checks in with her office every two hours or less. She has a car phone. Her office provides the staff with a trophy receptionist who phone-follows Mary Lou all over Anchorage with messages.

Recognizing that newspapers know what they are talking about, JM Tayler & Company invented a way of personalizing classified, plus stroking the egos of all the agents, over- and under-achievers alike. Now and then we printed headlines like:

AUDREY'S AWESOME NEW LISTING!

**ASK ASTRID
'BOUT HER 4 CONDOS**

JEAN JUST LISTED A BIG ESTATE

PETE DID IT AGAIN!

Since all the agents had a crack at seeing their names in print, those with floor duty were not unhappy about losing out on a few ad calls directed to specific coworkers.

Learn the Lingo

Travelers tell us that when they speak a few words of the local lingo in foreign lands, the natives become friendly. Learn some newspaper language. Your newspaper will appreciate your efforts. Friendly communication will be enhanced.

Here are some definitions gathered from the *Baltimore Sun:*

Agate Line: Standard unit of measurement for classified advertising space. 14 agate lines equal one inch.

Artwork: Photographs, illustrations, diagrams (not type).

Bold Type: Type that is in a heavier typeface than is normally used.

Bullets: Periods.

Camera Ready: Text, halftones, and graphics pasted in correct position and ready for reproduction.

Circulation: The number of copies printed by a publication. Circulation is measured on an average number of issues.

Column: The vertical arrangement of items on a newspaper page, usually separated by a black line or white space.

Column Inch: A space one column wide by one inch deep. A classified column inch equals 14 agate lines.

CPM: An acronym for "cost per thousand." The advertising cost to reach 1,000 adults.

Display Advertising: Ads that contain photographs, artwork, and/or large type. Display ads are typically more than one column wide, but not necessarily.

Edition: A complete press run of the newspaper.

Exclams: Exclamation points.

Facing Pages: Any two pages that face each other.

Flush Left: Type that is aligned on the left side of the ad.

Flush Right: Type that is aligned on the right side of the ad.

Font: An assortment of type for one size and style.

Headline: Type, usually larger than the body copy, that serves as attention getter.

In-Column Ad: An ad that does not exceed one column in width and contains no borders or artwork.

Justified Type: Type that is aligned along both the left and right edges.

Kill Order: The cancellation of an ad.

Layout: A sketch that gives the idea of a finished ad.

Leading: The vertical white space between lines of type, usually measured in points.

Light Face: Type that is thin. More likely used as body copy.

Line: The abbreviated term for agate line.

Logo: The identification symbol of a business.

Newsprint: Paper that is made from ground wood pulp.

Pasteup: The assembly of all parts of an ad. The headline, body copy, and art are all put into their exact position ready for reproduction.

Pica: A unit of measure used in printing. Six picas equal one inch.

Pickup: An ad that has appeared in the newspaper once and is being reused in a different edition.

Point: Unit of measure used in printing; 72 points equal one inch. Points also refer to the size of type.

Proof: Reproduction of an original ad that can be corrected prior to publication.

Rate Holder: An ad that is published to fulfill an advertising contract's minimum number of lines or column inches.

Reset: To do over again, to correct type.

Set: The width of the body of a piece of type.

Set Solid: Ad copy that is set in the smallest possible type with minimum leading.

Signature: The name, address, and phone number of a business.

TMC: An acronym for a "total market coverage" newspaper product, which includes subscribers and nonsubscribers.

Typeface: A design for a set of letters and numerals.

White Space: The area in an ad that contains neither type nor art.

Zoned Edition: Editions of a newspaper that are delivered to specific geographic areas.

My "civilian" friend Pete Mahler of North Carolina has sold everything from hogs to boats to houses, good times and bad, with dynamite classified advertising. His ads are anything but plain vanilla.

He has been known to print ads upside down. Sorry, I can't find newspaper language for "please print upside down."

Don't Blame Classified

It seems to real estate practitioners that newspapers are continually punching out the real estate industry despite the fact that classified real estate advertising is one of their biggest sources of revenue: "R. E. Firm Goes Belly Up," "Realty Agent Nabbed with Pot."

Newspapers have an annoying habit of reviewing do-it-yourself books on selling real estate. One particularly threatening feature article appeared in the local newspaper much to the alarm of real estate agents. In this article, written by a former realty agent, readers were advised not to pay commission, not to deal with "greedy" real estate practitioners. It was very insulting. The article went on to give readers in-depth information on how to go about selling without a professional. (JM Tayler & Company Realtors may have provoked this industry bashing. The author of that odious article was soundly rejected some years before when he came to JM Tayler & Company asking to join our sales force. His primary goal, he revealed, was to buy real estate for his personal investment portfolio. Our company would not hire any sales agent who intended to compete with our customers. This investor wolf in agent's clothing would have had first crack at the best properties.)

In retaliation, one of the local brokers called a boycott of the newspaper. He and some other brokers withdrew their advertising, for a week or two. The boycott was unsuccessful.

Do not blame the classified department for what gets printed on the editorial pages. It is not responsible for editorial policy.

Stay Loyal to Classified

It has become almost tradition that newspapers raise classified rates every couple of years. Newspapers are subject to increases in the cost of newsprint, litigation, labor strikes. Other advertising vehicles are subject to similar cost increases. Customers always take the fall.

During a mini-recession in the early 1980s, a group of San Francisco real estate heavies marched on their major newspaper. They demanded that their increased rates be lowered. They threatened to move their advertising to another newspaper. The major newspaper did not acquiesce. The heavies and many of their peers moved their advertising to a small city newspaper. The small newspaper thrived. But after a couple of years, one by one their customers moved back to the major newspaper. The small newspaper folded.

Then the heavies went into the advertising business together with the Board of Realtors. They published a real estate magazine that they dispensed free of charge in metal boxes on street corners next to the major newspapers' metal boxes. Metal boxes are still dispensing both the Realtors' magazine and the newspapers. All the real estate companies that advertise in the real estate magazine also advertise in the major newspaper.

Realty offices are deluged with new advertising ideas. Some have value. So far no new ideas have replaced classified newspaper advertising. The institution of classified newspaper advertising has been the "public's marketplace" in the United States for over 200 years. It has survived newspaper strikes, recession, depression, earthquakes, hurricanes, competition from the proliferation of other kinds of periodicals, from radio, from television, from computer technology, and from broker dissatisfaction. It still reaches the most people, in the shortest space of time, and, yes, for the least amount of money.

So, when you receive your next notice that rates are going up, go ahead, march into the classified office. But be nice. Don't hit on your pals at classified. The classified department does not set rate policy. The publisher sets rate policy. By all means, keep up the pressure on the publisher. Meanwhile, your classified buddies will be happy to help you modify your advertising, while maintaining your exposure, in order that you may stay within your budget.

By all means, keep up the pressure on the publisher, particularly when the real estate industry suffers bad times. Pressure the publisher to lower your classified rates for the duration of the bad times. Convince the publisher that, by making classified affordable, he will keep his valued real estate customers. Convince him that by putting in with the real estate industry, his classified section is not apt to shrink drastically, as it did in the early 1990s.

Give Helpful Hints

Your realty company is gracing the newspaper with exciting classified advertising. You are a friendly advertiser, a pleasure to work with. You don't rage at the rep when the paper makes boo-boos. This may be the time to suggest to the classified editor that the newspaper format needs some excitement added to it.

Nobody likes to be told how to run his business. But any supplier will listen to a good customer. Give the editor your ideas over lunch: How about a contest for the best ad of the month? How about more white space on the page? How about graphics to distinguish classifications, some cute little houses or some cows and piggies at the top of the urban property column? How about bringing in color for excitement? You can't afford it, but the newspaper can. How about holding more seminars for real estate customers? Maybe your news-paper would hire the gurus of real estate classified, Donn May (tel. 813-642-1869) or Tony Marsella (tel. 212-921-5080), to conduct those seminars.

To Agents

You probably won't have any direct contact with the newspaper, except to pass the time of day with the rep when she comes into the office to collect ad copy.

However, since you are intimately involved in the classified process, it would be well for you to know that process from soup to nuts. You will better appreciate deadlines and so will your sellers when you explain why the price change didn't make it into the Monday paper.

You will find, in this chapter, some valid excuses to give your seller for not advertising his condo in the *London Times* or *Trout Unlimited,* or for not being able to place his ad in the upper left-hand corner of the page.

5

Ya Gotta Systematize to Harvest Results

6

Say your real estate office is now turning out dynamite classified ad copy. Your newspaper buddies make it look good in print. Say the phones are ringing off the hook. But you're not pulling in any more new business than you did before. The reason is that your office is not yet prepared to harvest the results.

Be Prepared!

Systematize your office. The first system to prepare for harvesting is the telephone system. Fifty percent of ad calls into real estate offices are bungled:

"Hey, Honey, listen to this ad."

"Sounds like our dream house."

"Yep, it sure does. Hand me the phone."

Honey calls. But Casual Realty Company, which wrote the ad that interested Honey's hubby, dropped the ball. Darn it all, Honey hung up without making an appointment with a Casual agent or without giving her phone number or without giving her address, maybe even without waiting to speak to a Casual agent because:

1. Honey got impatient after four rings.
2. Casual Realty's phone was answered by voice mail or an answering service.
3. The receptionist sounded harassed or slurred.
4. Honey was put on hold for thirty seconds.
5. The floor person did not recognize the dream house Hubby had found in the paper.
6. The floor person didn't pull up the comparables.
7. The floor person was a chatterbox.
8. The floor person didn't ask for the order.

What a waste! Casual Realty Company could have made as much as $50,000 worth of commissions off that one ad call:

1. Purchase of the advertised dream house: $8,000.
2. Sale of Honey and Hubby's present home: $5,000.
3. Purchase of Honey and Hubby's next dream house: $12,000.
4. Sale of Honey and Hubby's first Casual Realty dream house: $10,000.
5. Sales to Honey and Hubby's friends: $15,000.

Please, don't let such disasters happen in your office. Get organized!

Install a practical phone system. Then create procedures to make your system work efficiently for you.

If you are purchasing a new phone system for your office, please buy a simple one, the simpler the better. Don't let your office technology junkies talk you into the latest, sophisticated, state-of-the-art, expensive equipment. The more "bells and whistles" you have, the more breakdowns and confusion you have to go with it. And what busy manager wants to spend time training new recruits and the "mechanically disinclined" to use functions they may never use?

The Sacred Phone

Consider installing a separate telephone line on the up desk with its very own number to be used only in advertising and on yard signs. Be sure to include the area code in your advertising if your ads draw calls from out of your area. Using an 800 number is better still.

Try to have the phone equipped with a distinctive ring. What an energizer! The office troops will stand to attention when they hear that distinctive ring-a-ding-dingie.

The up desk phone should be programmed so that it cannot accept interoffice calls. You don't want old George in the lunchroom buzzing the up desk during the floor person's opportunity call.

A lot of good ad calls come in after realty offices close up for the night, when breadwinners return home and open up the evening paper. Too many good after-hours calls are lost for lack of instant personal response. Realty offices generally switch their phones over to answering services that don't have any answers, onto voice mail, or into a message recording machine. (I cannot bear to discuss those hard-hearted real estate brokers who leave their poor little phones totally unattended after dark.)

Ad calls, day or night, are spontaneous, spur-of-the-moment calls. If a professional is not immediately available, the caller will quite spontaneously hang up. Even the most determined house hunter will hang up on an answering service, voice mail, or recording machine without leaving a message. They may move on to the competitors' ads that they've circled in the newspaper.

Call Forwarding at Your Service

There is a no-brainer telephone "bell and whistle" called *call forwarding,* which is a real handy-dandy tool for Realtors who want to collect prospects after hours.

This is a clever, easy-to-use function provided by the telephone company for very little money. It can be put into service immediately without any adjustment to office equipment. When activated, call forwarding redirects incoming calls to any location as programmed.

6

It works like this: The last person on the premises programs the up desk phone to transfer calls into a sales agent's home (not his tavern, please). He simply punches in a three-digit code and the sales agent's number. Then, when a call is made to the office, it rings into the sales agent's home. The caller is unaware of the transfer, unless, oops, a kiddy picks up the phone.

Warning: Teenagers hate it when "Dad or Mom has the duty." The phone is off-limits that night. Also, it could happen that call forwarding brings in painful middle-of-the-night wake-up calls. A Persian client of ours made several such wake-up calls from strange airports during his escape from the Ayatollah. My own dear mother aroused a salesman's family at 2:00 A.M. She was in Spain and reversed the time difference in her mind. (That's when JM Tayler & Company ordered a separate sacred advertising phone with its very own separate, secret-from-moms number.)

Incidentally, "Agent on Duty 24 Hours a Day" makes dynamite ad copy!

Spotlight Your Up Desk

The up desk is a very important workstation manned by a sales agent. It operates as a customer service center and new business headquarters.

Many offices do not treat the up desk with suitable respect. Rather, the floor person, the agent assigned to receive inquiries, is permitted to work from his own desk where he busies himself making personal calls and tending to his own paperwork. Obviously, hanging out in the privacy of one's own desk does not keep a floor person alert to incoming ad calls. Nor is the floor person "Johnny on the spot" when prospects walk in the door.

By all means, have a proper up desk and require floor people to sit there.

Position the up desk near reception so that the floor person can greet walk-ins. Put the up desk fairly close to the receptionist's station so the receptionist can signal the floor person when a call comes in or a walk-in approaches (but not close enough for chatting).

Recommendation: Do not place a side chair by the up desk. Otherwise, for sure, your floor person will be distracted by visiting office chums who settle down for a bit of chew-the-fat.

Stocking the Up Desk

Stock the up desk with tools of the floor person's trade:

1. **Ad Schedule Book**
2. **In-House Listing Book**
3. **Multiple Listing Book**
4. **Computer Terminal**
5. **Daily Bulletin**
6. **Blank Info Forms**
7. **Call Report Log**
8. **Newspaper**
9. **Telephone Directory**
10. **Local Map**

1. Ad Schedule Book: In this binder, the floor person finds copies of all classified ads scheduled for the current week and the past week. (Ads sometimes remain stuck to the refrigerator door for days until someone gets the urge to call.) The schedule needs to include the addresses of the properties and the names of the respective listing agents.

2. In-House Listing Book: This book provides quick access information about the company's own listings. It also includes information materials such as copies of multiple listing profile sheets and statements (in case the caller is really turned on).

3. **Multiple Listing Book:** Ad callers seldom purchase the home they've read about in the paper. (Shhh. Don't tell your sellers.) So be prepared to "bait and switch" your callers to other properties. The multiple listing book, which shows six to twelve properties at a glance, is another valuable quick reference tool.

Judy was the agent on duty. She received an ad call from a family newly arrived from Japan. She took the family to see the million-dollar house they called about. She persuaded them to see another million-dollar house nearby that she picked out of the MLS book. The Japanese family bought that one.

Mr. Stewart flew in from Australia. He bought a local newspaper at the airport. He rented a car. He drove directly to the real estate office with the paper folded back at the rental section. The floor person showed him rentals that first day. The second day, she showed him rental houses and houses for sale. The third day, Mr. Stewart ratified a purchase agreement in the departure lounge of the international airport.

4. **Computer Terminal:** The fastest way to access multiple listing information is by punching up comparables (comps) on the computer screen or by asking the computer to match up properties with the caller's want list. Floor persons will be ever-so-grateful for one of these on the up desk.

5. **Daily Bulletin:** The daily bulletin, to which everyone contributes, is a now-hear-this brief reporting of the latest real estate news. It's a way that scurrying sales agents talk to one another:

    A. Competitors' pocket listings
    B. FSBOs (for-sale-by-owner properties)
    C. Latest in-house sales
    D. New in-house listings
    E. Price changes
    F. Meetings

DAILY BULLETIN

DATE	AGENT	INFORMATION	PROPERTY ADDRESS	PRICE

Okay to copy—be my guest.

119

G. Agents' birthdays

H. How 'bout real estate gossip?...

6. **Blank Info Forms:** The daily bulletin is a great communicator, but agents need more than brief reporting to be able to sell pocket listings and FSBOs. The floor person and other office sleuths fill out info forms with pertinent facts about such properties, then make copies for all the other sales agents in the office. Keep a folder of these infos, in the up desk next to the company inventory list and the MLS book.

Stacks of home finding and home listing questionnaires in the up desk are helpmates for the floor person who wishes to take good notes while speaking to ad callers.

7. **Call Report Log:** Management, copywriters, listing agents, and sellers will want to know how the ads are pulling. The up desk log, on which the floor person reports calls and walk-ins, is their monitor.

In addition to keeping track of advertising, the log has other uses. For instance, it can be a great "brag book" in listing presentations. It will impress a buyer with the company that is so on-top-of-it. It may even be used as a Godzilla seller appeaser:

Once an enraged attorney threatened to yank his listing from JM Tayler & Company because of the "silly" ad we wrote about his house. Silly it was, too. The ad talked of blue jays, squirrels, "silver bells and cockle shells and pretty maids all in a row." The attorney's house was an add-on horror. We could not say it was enchanting, or even nice. So we raved about the enchanting country garden instead. Our listing was saved by the log. Floor persons, those good guys, had recorded twenty calls on that one ad. When shown the log, Mr. Monster Attorney calmed down. Then he demanded that the silly ad be run continuously until his (horrible) house was sold.

8. **Newspaper:** The floor persons should be "required" to search out pocket listings and FSBOs in the newspaper every day for the

PROPERTY INFORMATION

Address_____

Cross St._____

Lot #_____Size_____Block_____Tract_____Parcel#_____

Style_____Age_____

Detached_____Condo_____Coop_____

1st FL: BRs_____Bths_____LR_____DR_____Kit_____Other_____

2nd Fl: BRs_____Bths_____Other_____

Heat_____Frpl_____Security_____Bsmt_____

Roof_____Parking_____

Loan Info: Balance_____Mo. Payment_____

Lender_____

Price Includes_____

Remarks_____

_____

_____

_____

_____

_____

_____

_____

Show Instruct._____Comm._____

Listing Office_____

Owner/Occupant_____

Owner Address_____Tel#_____

Home Info Credit To_____(Company Agt.) Date_____

Okay to copy—be my guest.

121

HOME FINDING INITIATION QUESTIONNAIRE

CONFIDENTIAL   Approved_____

```
┌─────────────────────────────────────────────────────────────┐
│                                                             │
│                                                             │
│                                                             │
│                                                             │
│                                                             │
│                                                             │
└─────────────────────────────────────────────────────────────┘
```

Initial Contact by_____ Date_____

Assigned to_____ Date_____

Referred by_____

    Phone #_____ Address_____

    Fee_____ _____

Name of Prospect_____ Spouse_____

Home phone_____ Business phone_____

                                  Spouse's_____

Present Home Address _____

Name of Business_____Spouse's_____

HOUSING NEEDS:

STYLE	BR	BTH	FR	DR	POOL	GAR	AGE

Children _____

Preferred Location_____ Moving Date_____

Price Range $_____ Down Payment $_____

Present Home Sold?_____ Equity_____

Preferred PITI_____

COMMENTS:

RESULTS:

122

LISTING INITIATION QUESTIONNAIRE

CONFIDENTIAL   Approved_____

Initial Contact by_____Date_____

Assigned to_____ Date_____

Referred by_____ Date_____

    Phone #_____   Address_____

    Fee_____   _____

Property Owner_____   Spouse_____

Home Phone_____   Business Phone_____

                                                         Spouse's_____

Property Address_____

STYLE	BR	BTH	FR	DR	POOL	GAR	AGE

Loan Amount (1st)_____   Lender_____

        (2nd) _____   Lender_____

COMMENTS:

RESULTS:

Date_____

By_____

9-83

Okay to copy—be my guest.

FLOOR PERSON'S LOG

DATE	FL. PERSON	PROPERTY	TYPE CLIENT			RESPONDED TO			PROSPECT	AGENT
			PURCH	LIST	RENT	WALK-IN	SIGN	AD		

Okay to copy—be my guest.

benefit of the whole office. (If your salespeople tend to get mesmerized by the sports section, then put only the classified section on the up desk.)

9. Telephone directory: You don't want your floor persons to be using the phone directory to make outgoing calls, but you do want them to be able to check out callers in the directory. And, since ad callers have a way of asking Realtors all manner of questions, your floor person can better play "information booth" with a telephone directory near at hand.

10. Local map: Ad callers sometimes need explicit directions to your office or to your Sunday opens. Out-of-towners often ask the "information booth" directions to every place they are visiting that day.

More Tools

Unless your up desk is as big as a conference table, you will need another location for additional floor person tools-of-the-trade. You probably have some sort of "resource center" that includes a library of real estate books.

Your resource center should include the following client-background, private-eye-type resources:

1. *Haines Reverse Directory*
2. *Realdex*
3. *Map Books*

1. *Haines Reverse Directory:* The *Haines Reverse Directory* pertains to telephones. It puts a name and address to every listed phone number within certain code areas.

2. *Realdex:* The *Realdex,* preferably on microfiche because the Realdex books can be huge and cumbersome, gives information on all properties in each county such as original selling prices, number of rooms, and mortgages. The information is categorized by owner's name, street name, and/or parcel number. (Some very sophisticated realty boards are disseminating this kind of information via computer terminals.)

3. **Map books:** Great big floppy nail-breaking map books show lot lines, topography, dimensions, easements, etc.

By using these private-eye tools, a floor person can start a healthy dossier on his ad caller, or at least find out if he is "for real."

Prepare for Walk-Ins

Not all potential clients who are motivated by classified real estate ads make contact by phone. Some will go directly to the realty office, newspaper in hand.

In one way, walk-ins offer a greater potential for business than telephoners because they make a greater effort in responding to advertising.

Make walking into your office easy to do. Don't let a prospect veer off because your office does not look welcoming or because your entrance is obscure. Pay attention to:

1. **Signage**
2. **Front Entrance**
3. **Visible Insides**
4. **Reception Area**

1. Be sure your **sign** can be seen from the street and sidewalk. People feel uneasy entering any building for the first time. Guide visitors in with bold signage so they don't have time to think again.

2. Be sure the **front entrance** can be seen from the street and sidewalk. Show off your entrance with fresh paint, good lighting, an awning, or planters.

There is a funeral parlor in San Mateo, California, that has done a land office business for two generations. While a funeral parlor has to be the most forbidding of all business establishments, this funeral parlor is one of the most welcoming establishments in that town. What makes it welcoming is the front garden, which is always abloom with a thousand colorful plants.

3. Make as much of the **inside** of your office **visible** from the outside as possible. People feel more secure making that initial visit to an office if they can see what they are walking into. The more glass the better, particularly by the front door.

4. Be sure the **reception area** is comfortable. Furnish it with plenty of seating. Stock it with a variety of current magazines and some examples of your best marketing materials. (Don't put out any materials that feature your competitors' listings, or your walk-ins may be sitting in the competitor's reception area tomorrow.)

Don't install one of those formidable high counters that divide reception areas from the rest of the office, like the counters in law offices. You're not in the intimidation business. While such counters might shelter the receptionist from the breezes and hide clutter, they don't say to walk-ins, "Come in, come in. You're welcome here."

Hire a Trophy Receptionist

Your receptionist is the gateway to your company, often the public's first contact with your office. If your receptionist is articulate, cheerful, mannerly, has good grammar, and responds with the immediacy required by the residential real estate business, that receptionist can increase your bottom line 10 percent all by herself.

McKinsey Company, one of the world's great management consulting firms, taught me the importance of a trophy receptionist long before I was in a position to hire one. I had called McKinsey to make an appointment with my buyer. Though I identified my call as personal, the articulate voice on the other end handled my call with

6

utmost courtesy and efficiency. When I arrived at the McKinsey offices for my appointment, I was received by the owner of that articulate voice. (She was a beautiful "African Princess" dressed in native Kinte cloth.) She greeted me and all the other walk-ins as visiting royalty. She had been taught the value of good public relations, even with those who are not company clients. It was obvious that this trophy receptionist was part of the powerful McKinsey business promotion team.

Everyone loved Wendy, our JM Tayler & Company trophy. She, too, treated callers and walk-ins like royalty. She recognized our clients' voices and called them by name. Wendy was such a team player that she would phone-follow our agents all over the county with messages. She knew where the ladies had their hair done. She knew where the gents worked out. She had full charge of the phone system. She trained our new troops on how to operate the system. She approved the phone bills. She fattened our bottom line.

Be aware that such trophy receptionists are not recruited by the low wage scale customarily, foolishly, budgeted for that particular position.

What, No Receptionist?

Small realty offices might not have a receptionist, trophy or otherwise. An all-purpose secretary does the clerical and escrow work and answers the phones too, poor thing.

If there is no receptionist at your firm, then it is crucial that you have a separate sacred advertising phone on your up desk, with a separate sacred number. Incoming ad calls bypass the main phone line and the all-purpose secretary who has more than enough work to do. Ad calls are picked up directly by the floor person, thereby ensuring that opportunity calls are answered before the fourth ring, that ad callers are not put on hold, and that service is immediate.

Do not even think of putting an answering service, voice mail, or a recording machine on that sacred line. Ad callers expect, and should receive, the courtesy of a real-live person in attendance to receive their response, which was solicited in the first place by the company that placed the ad in the newspaper.

One Saturday, with investment in mind, I called about a house that was advertised by a national company in their very immodest half-page ad (cost about $10,000). An answering service picked up the phone. "They're out to lunch," I was told. All thirty of them? I'll say they were "out to lunch."

Next morning, I called on another company's expensive half-page ad. Voice mail picked up. Another realty company was "out to lunch." Tsk, tsk. Such lack of systematization, and public service, will never do.

To Agents

Don't say, "Forget it. It's not my job to organize the office." 'Tis too your job if management is too overworked to follow through with the ideas presented in this chapter. You could volunteer to set up the up desk for the office. You could set up the reception area yourself. Be a hero. Some of the best systems at JM Tayler & Company Realtors were contributed by the sales agents and were received with gratitude.

Or you can just stick to your own knitting by fixing yourself a mini portable up desk in your brief case. Stuff it with up desk goodies like the ad schedule, the company inventory list, your multiple listing book, and home finding and home listing forms.

Training the Troops

7

This is the tough chapter for managers. Training adults is a real challenge to one's leadership abilities.

Political Science

For want of strategic planning, some of the greatest business innovations have remained glued to the printed page. Some of the greatest training programs are still locked up in their manuals. Avoid this expensive waste.

Just as we identify our winning classified advertising program, including systematizing the office, so must we identify the opposition to the program. The opposition is the old guard in the office, in every office, that is resistant to new tricks. The opposition is the superstars, prima donnas who vehemently oppose anything that might steal time away from their precious deals. These opposers have the power to call a general strike in the office.

7

So if you are determined that classified will do, for your office, all that it is capable of, first bring the powerhouses on board.

Here is the management strategy, not born of the Wharton School of Business, that has worked for me every time I needed to shake up my office: Before you announce the new program, call a meeting of the old guard and the prima donnas. Give the potential opponents an overview of your program. Ask for comments. You will get some good ideas. These are savvy characters.

Ask them to volunteer to teach part of the training classes. Being involved in teaching will get the know-it-alls to accept training as nothing else can. Now your program becomes theirs. Not only will your leaders sell it to the rest of the office, they will act as its master sergeants. They will monitor performance for you. They will bug co-workers who falter at the up desk.

Motivated Opening

Commence your training session with a real "hip-hip-hooray" introduction. Wow your trainees with the benefits they are to receive from classified advertising. Tell them that once they've learned the process, they can increase their production by 20 percent. (Some of the Tayler sales agents reported that a third of their production came from the up desk.)

Our super saleswoman Betsy White did twelve transactions, including two million-dollar sales, all originating from just one up call. Throw in some of your own local success stories. Put pants on your promises by quoting some statistics from chapter 1. Give history. Give newspaper circulation figures.

Manning the Up Desk

Once you have the troops all fired up, take them in manageable groups to your retrofitted up desk. Describe the up desk as their very own "New Business Center." You and/or a prima donna co-trainer show them each of the ten handy-dandy aids, one by one, that they will be using (see page 117). Demonstrate their use.

Put on a little performance. You and/or a superstar co-trainer play the floor person.

Mommy Call
Pick up the phone.

"Hello, this is Harold."

Pause.

"No, ma'am, that home is not within walking distance of an elementary school."

Open the company listing book. Open the multiple listing book.

"But there are several nice homes for sale near Brookbank Elementary."

Pause.

"Since those two seem to fit the bill, may I show them to you now before the boys get home from school?"

Bachelor Call
Pick up the phone.

"No, sir, that particular condominium does not have a swimming pool."

Turn on the computer terminal.

"There are other condos that have pools, however. Here's one that has a tennis court as well."

Take out a home finding questionnaire.

Seller Call
Pick up the phone.

"It's no problem at all, madame. I am happy to tell you what's sold in your neighborhood."

Turn on the computer.

7

"I have a list of eight comparable homes here, which have sold during the past year. I will drop the list off at your house on my way home."

Take out a home listing questionnaire.

When they catch on, maybe your less inhibited trainees can be tapped for more role-playing.

Doing-the-Paper

Next introduce "doing-the-paper" to your trainees. Explain that doing-the-paper is a simple and time-effective method of distributing important information to everyone in the office about competitors' "hip pocket listings" (those not shared through multiple listing service) and FSBOs (properties for sale by owners).

Tell them that doing-the-paper will provide them with more good properties to sell. Tell them that agents who work for realty offices that do-the-paper really come across to the public as knowing their stuff.

Take out of the up desk some doing-the-paper tools. Show your trainees a mock-up tear sheet from classified. Beforehand you have noted in green ink the street names of all the properties in your market area that you know to be in MLS. You have written in red the addresses of the properties not in MLS (the pocket listings and FSBOs) across the ads.

It is the floor person's job to identify MLS listings in green (with help from the multiple listing book), and non-MLS listings in red (by calling the phone numbers given in the paper).

At the onset, this will look like an all-day job to your troops. It isn't, because old tear sheets are kept in the up desk, so that the next floor person on duty can refer to the former's marked-up tear sheets. Therefore, no floor person starts from scratch.

Bring out the daily bulletin and a stack of info forms. Tell the class that the floor persons write on the bulletin a brief report of the non-

FORMBY **Offers in region of £250,000**
THIS OUTSTANDING ARCHITECT DESIGNED RESIDENCE HAS A DELIGHTFUL WOODED REAR GARDEN AND IS QUIETLY SITUATED WITHIN A FEW MINUTES WALK OF FORMBY VILLAGE AND ALL AMENITIES; exceptionally spacious accommodation; hall, fitted cloaks, 2 separate entertaining [illegible], family room, large kitchen/dining area, master bedroom with en-suite bathroom, 4 further bedrooms, second bathroom; ample parking, double garage; built to a first class specification with innumerable refinements; a fine property of distictive design and quality.

FORMBY **£245,000**
Standing in lawned and wooded gardens, extending to approx ½ acre, a spacious and individual detached residence, designed to take full advantage of the [illegible] southerly rear aspect; exceptional accommodation; [illegible] cloakroom, 2 separate entertaining rooms [illegible] patio doors, kitchen/family dining room, 5 double bedrooms, bathroom, shower room; double garage; gas central heating; double glazing; convenient for schools, station and shops; an individually designed family residence in a delightful setting.

BARKFIELD AVENUE, FORMBY **£245,000**
A FINE DETACHED CHARACTER RESIDENCE IN MATURE AND SECLUDED GARDENS OF ALMOST ONE-THIRD OF AN ACRE IN FIRST CLASS SITUATION; elegant lounge with beamed ceiling, dining room, family room, kitchen/breakfast room with quality fittings, [illegible], ground floor study or bedroom and ground floor bathroom and wc, on first floo there are 4 bedrooms, bathroom and wc; 4-car garage; gas central heating; tastefully decorated and refurbished throughout; inspection strongly recommended.

FRESHFIELD **£245,000**
An exceptional detached residence, situated in one of the best residential areas of Freshfield, luxuriously appointed throughout and standing in delightful gardens, planted with many lovely shrubs and trees; particularly spacious and [illegible] easily managed accommodation; of charming dining hall, fitted cloakroom, magnificent drawing room with doors to delightful south westerly facing conservatory, splendid family room, [illegible] superb kitchen/breakfast room, laundry, [illegible] feature fine staircase, fine master bedroom with built-in furnishings and en-suite bathroom, 3 further bedrooms, 2nd bathroom; gas central heating; carriage sweep drive, double garage, caravan place; an outstanding property with numerous refinements and opportunity to acquire a home of distinction of a calibre rarely available.

FORMBY **£210,000**
A superior detached residence [illegible] Messrs Trumans Limited, quietly situated convenient for the village; deceptively spacious accommodation; [illegible]; fitted cloaks, lounge, dining room, family room, [illegible] fitted kitchen/breakfast area, master bedroom built in furnishings and en suite luxury bathroom; gas central heating, cavity insulation, double glazing, 2 car garage, attractively laid out gardens; high standard of appointments; a splendid, modern family home.

OFF WICKS LANE, FORMBY **£202,500**
A choice detached residence occupying a particularly quiet situation, in an excellent residential area; enjoying a southerly rear aspect, this delightful residence is appointed to a high standard and the particularly spacious accommodation includings a fitted cloakroom, a fine through lounge with hole-in-the-wall fireplace and patio doors to terrace, separate dining room, study or fifth bedroom, a splendid kitchen/dining room with extensive regency fittings, laundry, master bed with "Sharps" furnishings and en-suite lusury shower room, 3 further beds, fully tiled bathroom with corner bath; refinements including double glazed hardwood framed windows, panel doors, brass fittings; gas central heating; double garage; laid out gardens; decorated to a light tasteful scheme, this immaculate family residence is strongly recommended.

FORMBY **£189,500**
An exceptional detached residence, enjoying a secluded southerly aspect overlooking an outstanding and superbly laid out garden; luxuriously appointed throughout, adaptable accommodation; of magnificent [illegible] southfacing entertaining [illegible] dining room, fully fitted [illegible], laundry, study or [illegible] bedrooms, luxury shower room, 3 bathrooms, bathroom [illegible] central heating; 2 car garage, ample parking space [illegible] for schools, transport, pinewoods; an immaculate residence and recommended.

BLUNDELLSANDS **£187,500**
Immaculate character detached true bungalow, in excellent situation convenient for Rugby and Golf clubs, good shopping and Liverpool/Southport electric railway; deceptively spacious centrally heated accommodation; [illegible] with beamed ceiling, dining room, [illegible] extensively [illegible] kitchen/breakfast room, laundry, 4 bedrooms, study or 5th bedroom, 2 bathrooms; garage, lovely mature gardens of interest to garden lovers; a unique property and inspection recommended.

HIGHTOWN **£187,000**
A charming detached residence of considerable character, tastefully refurbished in a first class residential position; bright and spacious centrally heated accommodation; reception hallway, delightful lounge, elegant dining room, attractive study/living room, Elizabeth Ann kitchen/breakfast room, laundry, 4 bedrooms, well appointed bathroom, double garage, ample parking, attractively laid out gardens; innumerable refinements and features.

PHILLIPS LANE, FORMBY **£135,000**
PLEASANTLY SITUATED CLOSE TO FORMBY PARK AND WITH A DELIGHTFUL SOUTHERLY REAR ASPECT OVERLOOKING A LOVELY GARDEN OF INTEREST TO GARDEN LOVERS

An immaculate detached residence; hall, 2 separate entertaining rooms, spacious kitchen/breakfast area, 4 bedrooms, bathroom; gas central heating; garage; excellent decorative order.

FORMBY **£58,500**
IDEAL FOR FIRST TIME BUYERS

A compactly planned, centrally heated modern house; vestibule, spacious lounge/dining room, kitchen, 2 beds, bathroom; garage; gardens; good decorative order; recommended.

FORMBY **£84,500**
AN EXCEPTIONAL AND BEAUTIFULLY APPOINTED SEMI-DETACHED BUNGALOW WITH SOUTHERLY ASPECT OVERLOOKING A PLEASANT GARDEN

Refurbished to a high standard; hall, charming lounge with french door to sunny terrace, spacious well appointed kitchen/dining room with split level cooker etc, 2 double bedrooms, well appointed bathroom with champagne suite; gas central heating; uPVC double glazing; room for garage; tastefully decorated; "an easily managed bungalow — convenient for all amenities.

PARADISE LANE, FRESHFIELD **£136,000**
CHARMING COTTAGE STYLE RESIDENCE, IMMACULATE AND RECENTLY COMPREHENSIVELY MODERNISED TO HIGH STANDARD

Hall, 2 separate entertaining rooms, model kitchen with extensive fittings and split-level cooker, bright landing with writing area, master bedroom, luxury en-suite shower room, 3 further double bedrooms, family bathroom with shower compartment; gas central heating; ample parking for caravan; double garage; established gardens with secluded westerly rear garden; a delightful family home.

FRESHFIELD **Offers in region of £180,000**
THIS CHOICE DETACHED RESIDENCE OCCUPIES A PARTICULARLY PLEASANT SITUATION CLOSE TO VICTORIA ROAD AND WITHIN A FEW MINUTES WALK OF THE NATURE TRUST PINEWOODS; deceptively spacious accommodation with gas central heating and double glazing; fine [illegible] lounge with feature fireplace and patio [illegible] lovely garden, separate L shaped dining room, [illegible] kitchen with light oak unit, laundry, shower room, 5 bedrooms, fully tiled bathroom; parking for several cars, double garage; well screened rear garden with numerous shrubs and trees; a spacious family property and recommended.

SANDY LANE, HIGHTOWN **Offers in region of £177,500**
A delightful detached cottage style residence of considerable charm, standing in secluded and mature gardens; excellent centrally heated accommodation; attractive hall, beamed ceiling, fitted cloaks, 2 excellent entertaining rooms, [illegible] bathroom, large kitchen, laundry, 4 bedrooms (2 [illegible] and b.i.w's), bathroom and wc, second wc; 2-car garage; a family home of a type rarely available.

FORMBY **£175,000**
Choice detached residence used as Porchester show house with innumerable refinements, tasteful decor and fittings; excellent centrally heated accommodation; hall, fitted cloaks, elegant lounge archway to dining room, splendid [illegible], with extensive medium oak [illegible], laundry, master bed with en-suite luxury shower room, 3 further bedrooms, second bathroom; landscaped gardens with numerous shrubs, secluded westerly aspect; ample parking; convenient for schools, transport; a fine modern family property.

FRESHFIELD **Offers in region of £175,000**
Fine residence in one-third of an acre with potential for re-development; detached character residence with frontage of [illegible] and potential for redevelopment [illegible] dwellings; [illegible] tremendous scope for modernisation of pleasing [illegible] house with 3 entertaining rooms, [illegible] bedrooms and good sized gardens; details on request.

MERSEY AVENUE, FRESHFIELD **Offers in region of £170,000**
A choice detached bungalow, affording spacious accommodation and occupying a pleasant position in a quiet cul-de-sac, close to Freshfield station; centrally heated and double-glazed throughout; the accommodation includes hall, delightful lounge, dining room, conservatory, breakfast room, utility room, family room or study, 3 good bedrooms, bathroom, further accommodation to first floor; mature well screened gardens; garage.

CLOSE TO FRESHFIELD STATION **£168,500**
Beautifully appointed detached residence with wooded and secluded rear garden; fitted cloakroom, elegant lounge, dining room, attractive conservatory, study, spacious L-shaped kitchen/dining area with cooker and extensive fittings, [illegible] bedrooms [illegible] wardrobes, luxury bathroom; ample parking, large [illegible]; exceptional interior decoration; an immaculate family home and recommended.

FRESHFIELD **£166,000**
Well appointed detached house, in quiet situation and yet convenient station, bus routes and schools; thoughtfully extended and tastefully refurbished; hall, bright through lounge, dining room, family room, beautifully appointed kitchen, utility, fitted cloaks, 4 bedrooms, [illegible] extensive built-in furnishings, [illegible] jacuzzi; gas central heating, ample parking, garage; secluded rear garden; a modern family home in immaculate order.

FORMBY **£165,000**
Occupying a particularly fine plot with southerly rear aspect, this detached residence is architect designed [illegible] owner; centrally heated accommodation, [illegible] southerly rear aspect, [illegible] fitted cloaks, lounge [illegible] window overlooking the rear garden, dining room, kitchen/breakfast area, 3 bedrooms, studio or [illegible] bedroom, bathroom; ample parking; garage; convenient for transport, schools etc, abundantly stocked gardens of interest to garden lovers; easily managed and individual home and recommended.

FORMBY **£155,000**
Close to station and set in a particularly spacious family residence [illegible] large southfacing rear garden; hall, 2 separate entertaining rooms, breakfast room, fully fitted kitchen, laundry, 4 good bedrooms, bathroom, [illegible] suite; gas central heating; double glazing, double garage, a larger than average [illegible] family house and recommended.

CHURCH ROAD, FORMBY **£155,000**
An excellent detached character residence; with large westerly facing rear garden and conveniently situated for schools, bus, village; [illegible] hall, lounge, dining room, 3rd entertaining room, excellent kitchen/breakfast area, well fitted shower room, 4 good bedrooms, bathroom; 2-car garage; ample parking; larger than average gardens, abundantly stocked; a splendid family home.

BUTTERMERE CLOSE **£155,000**
An immaculate detached dormer bungalow with spacious accommodation, adaptable to individual requirements and particularly well furnished throughout; delightful through entertaining room [illegible] 2ft 6in long, with [illegible] slate fireplace, well fitted kitchen/family dining room with extensive fittings, 4 bedrooms, fully tiled bathroom, [illegible] shower room; gas central heating; upvc double glazing; double garage; secluded and abundantly stocked landscaped gardens; many features and inspection recommended.

Tear sheet

MLS properties they've found (and all the other meaty real estate news they've heard).

Tell the class that the floor person fills out info forms with more complete data, the kind of data that sales agents need in order to show the properties. Then the floor person copies the filled-out info forms and distributes them to the whole office, like a good boy. Emphasize that the data must include the commission that the FSBO is willing to pay.

Eons ago, when I was a naive new licensee, I called on a FSBO ad. I asked the owner if I might show his home. He agreed. I asked if he would "cooperate." He said he would. So I showed the house. My clients liked it. I wrote up an offer. The seller accepted the offer. He signed the deposit receipt, but not until he had crossed out my commission. I protested. "You told me you would cooperate!" "I did," he said. "I let you show my house to your friends." Well, my "friends" were very thankful, but not thankful enough to list that same house with me after their cousin came into the real estate business several years later.

Trainers be warned. Sales agents tend to think doing-the-paper is grunt work. Take heart; sales agents are quite willing to do that grunt work once they've sold a property off an info, or once they've earned a slice of commission (usually 10 percent) from the coworker who made a sale off his info. The slice is darn good wages for thirty minutes of grunt work.

Sales agents automatically become enthusiastic about doing-the-paper when it's a sellers' market, when inventory is scarce, when they are desperate for good properties to show.

The great industrialist Henry J. Kaiser had a motto, Find a Need and Fill It. Certain entrepreneurs have found the need to do-the-paper for realty offices where grunt work is not tolerated. These entrepreneurs hire their own simulated "floor persons" to do-the-paper. Every week they deliver, to their realty customers, packets of classified tear sheets on which they have identified the address of each and every property advertised in the local newspaper. (A couple of agents at JM Tayler & Company would have jumped at the chance to pay for such a service out of their very own pockets had it been available in our county.)

This service is a limited godsend service. Once a week is too much delay time in a warm to hot market. Conscientious realty offices will want to maintain daily in-house doing-the-paper at least during those glorious times when properties sell within three or four days.

Teach Telephone Techniques

It is not easy, I've found, to teach a group of adults something in which they feel proficient. "Hell, man, I've been using these damn things since Granny put a Fisher-Price toy phone in my playpen." It is particularly difficult when those adults are independent contractors. So you might consider bringing in the "authorities" to kick off your telephone techniques training. (I was having a conversation with my son Jay, then ten years old. "I already told you about that, sweetheart," I said. "I guess you did, Mom. But sometimes I tune you out.") Your telephone company may be willing to tune in your agents to telephone techniques at a sales meeting free of charge, or provide an inexpensive seminar.

You could hire one of those commercial companies that train employees to communicate effectively on the telephone. You will find them in the telephone directory under **telemarketing,** in their trade magazine *Inbound-Outbound,* or by contacting:

The American Telemarketing Association
444 North Larchmont Blvd., Suite 200
Los Angeles, CA 90004
(800) 441-3335

Don't you dare delegate the entire telephone techniques training to the "authorities" though. Their programs are terrific, but they are

7

generic. They may not address the variables of the residential real estate business. They certainly will not address the specifics of real estate classified advertising. Besides, who knows the needs of your business and ways of your employees as well as you?

When you take over with your own super-duper telephone techniques training, you'll no doubt want to repeat some of the "authorities'" most poignant advice in your own best real estate vernacular.

The authorities aren't real estate professionals, so be prepared to mop up. Some things they say you may want to countermand. That's another reason for having them go first, like having the competition present first at a simultaneous offer.

I attended a dynamic telephone techniques class at Pacific Bell in San Francisco. I had only one disagreement with the trainer, a disagreement that was shared by the trophy receptionists in my class.

Pac Bell preaches courtesy. They told us to say, when answering the phone, "May I help you?" or "Thank you for calling" after giving the company name. The trophies knew by experience that a tail comment is not expected. The caller is apt to start talking before the answerer is finished. In the theater that's called "stepping on his lines." This makes for an awkward stop/start beginning. We respectfully decided not to pick up on that one Pac Bell piece of advice.

The famous columnist Herb Caen complained about another kind of tail comment in the *San Francisco Chronicle*, March 22, 1993:

> *To phone ops who ask "How may I direct your call?" Sometimes I say, "In the style of Federico Fellini." Other times, "To the idiot who makes you say, 'How may I direct your call?' "*

And in his November 29, 1993, column:

> *I also note with distaste that evil employers still make their phone ops and receptionists ask the time-wasting and stuffy "How may I direct your call?" or "Thank you for calling the West Side Widget*

TELEPHONE TECHNIQUES
COURSE OUTLINE

Introduction
Your Role in Your Company is a Critical One: "Director of Public Relations"
How You Respond to a Customer Can Make or Break the Business Relationship

Foreword
Being the Best

Developing Professional Telephone Skills
Become the Person You Would Rather Talk To

What Your Voice Says About You
Put a Smile In Your Voice
Reduce Your Rate of Speech
Speak Directly Into the Telephone
Enunciate Your Words
Sound Natural
Listen to Your Own Voice
Consider Inflection

Good Telephone Manners – When You Receive A Telephone Call:
Be Prepared to Answer
Answer Promptly
Identify Yourself
Call the Person By Name
Use the Hold Feature Properly
Manage Call Interruptions
Transfer Calls Only When Necessary
Complete Calls Courteously
Make the Customer Feel Important

How to Manage The Difficult Customer
A Difficult Customer is a Golden Opportunity
Learn the Proper Steps

Use a Professional Vocabulary
Be Positive
Use Language They Understand

A PACIFIC TELESIS COMPANY / / / / / / **PACIFIC BELL.**

Reprinted with permission of Pacific Bell

Answering Calls For Others
Explain Co-Worker's Absence Appropriately
Screen Calls Tactfully
Take Accurate Messages

When You Place A Telephone Call
Plan Your Call In Advance
Time Your Call Carefully
Be Sure of the Telephone Number
Identify Yourself
Leave Complete Messages

Learning To Listen
When the Customer Starts Talking You Stop
Never Interrupt the Customer
Take Notes
Listen for Overtones
Limit Your Own Talking

Summary
The Eight Commandments of Effective Telephone Techniques

Appendix
A. Voice self-critique
B. Identifying yourself – Phrases (Incoming Calls)
C. Leaving the line and returning to the call – Phrases (Incoming and Outgoing Calls)
D. Transferring calls – Phrases (Incoming Calls)
E. Terminating the call – Phrases (Incoming and Outgoing Calls)
F. Screening calls – Phrases (Incoming Calls)
G. Roadblocks to effective listening

Company" before discovering that you have called to make a complaint. A simple identification is enough, honest.

Okay, Everybody into the Pool

Have your receptionist sit in on the telephone techniques classes. As a matter of fact, have anyone who might ever answer an incoming call in your office sit in, even your once-a-week bookkeeper.

Ask your prima donna co-trainers to pass out agendas of the subjects to be discussed in class. Agendas have a way of zapping the daydreamers, and squelching the chatty Cathies who like to monopolize class time.

You will have established the precise greeting that you expect everyone is to use when answering outside calls. Now's the time to make your exact greeting **company law.** It is to start out with "Good Morning" or "Good Afternoon." (In Hawaii it's "Aloha.") Then there is a pause and the company name is given. Another pause. Instruct your trainees: no "tails." Save those niceties for the floor person.

The company name must be no longer than eight syllables, or the caller could step on the answerer's lines. So if you have one of those double-barreled names like "The Montezuma County Residential Real Estate Company," shorten it to "Montezuma Real Estate."

By all means do not screen calls. It is offensive, certainly at realty offices, to ask the purpose of the call. If I telephone an accountant's office and I am asked the purpose of my call, I snap back "accountancy." Or if I am so queried when I call an attorney's office I am apt to answer "legalities."

When an ad call is redirected to the up desk, it must be picked up by the floor person within twenty seconds. Comedian George Carlin says, "Being put on hold is like being put in purgatory." If the floor person is outside sneaking a smoke, then the ad call is redirected to

7

another agent. Of course, boo-hoo, if that other agent scores, the floor person has lost a prospect.

The floor person who receives a redirected up call need not repeat "Good Morning." Giving a first name is sufficient. She must not identify herself as *Mrs.* So-and-so. This is utter pomposity, my dear. You don't want the ad caller to visualize you as one of those haughty real estate ladies with a Vuitton handbag who gets all of her business from the bridge table, none from the up desk.

The floor person should not push for the caller's name right off. He should wait until the caller has been sufficiently tenderized.

Say It, Loud and Clear

Much needs to be said, these days, about being heard over the telephone.

Before 1976, Ma Bell provided the whole country with uniform telephone service. We could count on about the same tone being transmitted over every instrument. Now there are over seventy different telephone systems operating in the United States, each manufactured somewhat differently. Each is subject to different tonal quality. In addition, there are hundreds of different kinds of instruments sold in phone stores: transparent phones, Mickey Mouse phones, multiple button consoles, cellular phones, phones wearing hula skirts with rhinestones for nipples. The different casings (and hula skirts) alone will alter voice tone.

Therefore, it is very important to initiate every telephone conversation with the utmost attention to being heard. It's a darn nuisance to ask people to repeat and repeat.

Here's a revealing little game your trainees can play. Give each a blind list of telephone numbers of ten different business offices. Have the agents call those numbers on their individual lists. As they call, they are to check the ones whose company name they could distinguish without having to ask that it be repeated. The dismal tally will be 50 percent, even lower if the list includes government offices. Your point will be made.

An important reason why real estate offices need to answer their phones "loud and clear" is that our country has become so international. Realty offices are receiving calls from people whose first language is not English. These people may be particularly ill at ease when speaking to strangers on the telephone. As radio listeners say when they call in on talk shows, "I'm nervous. I'm a first-time caller."

Telephones flatten out the voice. Ma Bell's did too. So agents need to put a lot more energy in their telephone voices than into their face-to-face voices. Otherwise, even our most articulate floor person may sound a bit of a dullard, or bored with his caller or his product.

At JM Tayler & Company Realtors there were two stars, both named Ann. Both had taken theater training. They scintillated so darn much over the up desk phone that coworkers got the giggles. That is, coworkers got the giggles until they caught on to the fact that the Anns scored on every up call.

Since not too many real estate agents have been to theater school, here are some helpful hints on how the rest of us can come off "bright eyed and bushy tailed" on the telephone:

1. Smile while you talk.
2. Gesture while you talk.
3. Stand, particularly when tired.
4. Look out the window at busy traffic.
5. Pretend you're on stage.
6. Look into a mirror while speaking.

Pacific Bell gives a mirrors to their students. On each mirror is printed, "What you see is what they hear."

Managers, mirrors might be nice table favors at your next office party...

7 The True Objective

If you stand before your class and ask, "What is the company's true objective in putting this here house ad in the newspaper?" your class will no doubt answer, "To sell the house" (ya dummy), and you will respond, "You're wrong!" (ya smart-ass kids).

Have you ever heard of a Realtor receiving a call that goes like this: "I read your ad in classified. I want to buy that house (sight unseen). Bring me a deposit receipt?" Ads don't sell houses. **People sell houses!**

The first and foremost true objective of classified real estate advertising is to make the phones ring. Once the classified ad has met the first and foremost true objective, the floor person takes over. The floor person works to achieve his own "first and foremost true objective," which is to gain an appointment with the ad caller, sooner or later. While the floor person talks ever so enthusiastically about the house advertised, and other company listings, he thinks, "I've got to get together with this caller so I can have a chance sell him something, anything, whenever." They know that callers seldom purchase the homes they call about.

Getting an appointment may take some cunning. The most serious home seekers or would-be sellers rarely intend to make appointments with agents the first time they make contact. So the sharpest of floor people may not be granted an appointment during that first conversation, or the next, or the next. It might take a year of phone conversations to land an appointment. Patience, my dears. The commissions are worth it.

I was sitting the floor one day. An ad call came in. The lady and I talked and talked. It became apparent that she was not a buyer or a seller. She was one of those mental types, a collector of knowledge. However, we became close telephone friends. I continued to have long telephone conversations with Susie for over a year before we met in person. Eventually I listed her house. Years later I attended her daughter's wedding in Camden, Maine. I profited. I earned a commission and a lifelong friend.

Score Card

Floor persons should consider their time on floor duty profitable, if they have:

1. Set up an appointment.

or

2. Got the caller's name, phone number, and address.

or

3. Got the caller's real name and phone number.

or

4. Got the caller's real name and address.

or

5. Got the caller's real name.

or

6. Just planted their own name and the company's name in the caller's mind.

If the floor person gets the appointment right off, Eureka! He scored big!

Floor persons will have lots of opportunity to score in the future if they've accomplished numbers 2 through 5. They can pat themselves on the back.

About number 6: If a floor person has really polished up his conversational skills, he will be remembered as a friendly, knowledgeable professional. He may very well receive a more productive phone call from that same caller or from the caller's friend months or even years later. We Americans move every five to eight years. So the pat on the back is always an eventuality.

There are memory tricks, called free association, that my father learned in Toastmasters. You can use them to plant your name with the caller:

1. If your name is Brown: "My name is Brown, like chocolate."
2. If your name is Woodhouse: "My name is Woodhouse; think of a log cabin."
3. If your name is Beard: "My name is Beard, you know, whiskers."
4. If your last name is unpronounceable: "My first name is Bob. My last name is unpronounceable." Chances are the next time the fellow calls in, he'll ask for the guy with the unpronounceable last name. If both your names are unpronounceable, you'd be smart to think up a memorable nickname. Put it on your business cards.

There are funny tales of free association memory tricks that have gone awry. Cousin Betsy once had an attorney named Mr. Stout. The slim gentleman is remembered by the family as Betsy's "Mr. Skinny."

Moment of Truth

There is a moment in every conversation when the ad caller has been sufficiently tenderized. Strike! The floor person scores.

Listen for excitement in the caller's voice. Listen for curiosity. Listen for the signs of fatigue, "Uh huh, uh huh." Then, zap, the floor person sets the hook:

"Let's go see."

"We could do a quick drive-by."

"I'll drop off the comparables at your house."

"I'll mail the information to your office."

"I'll call you when the new listings come out."

"Mustn't let it burn. Quick, what's your phone number?"

"I understand. Well, I've enjoyed our conversation. Please call me again."

"I Wanna Know About..."

When an ad call comes in, the floor person has to move fast, grab his handy-dandy up desk tools, and be ready to satisfy the ad caller's quest for information without pause. If the caller's first question doesn't meet with a satisfactory response, the caller is apt to think "phooie on youie" and hang up as fast as he can.

He's apt to hang up soon thereafter, anyway, if the floor person gives him too much information. The more details the caller gets about the property advertised, the more objections he may find to hang up about. The floor person wants to give just enough information to satisfy the caller's immediate curiosity, then add some enticements, so that the caller will want to see the property for himself.

Here's something that should be made company law: Never give out the property address over the phone. One may respond to the caller's demand for the address by saying, " I'm sorry. The sellers have instructed us not to give out the address over the phone. But they are most cooperative about letting us show it." Should you give out addresses to callers, they may not like the location and hang up. Or they may drive by the property and discount it from the exterior. Or they may ask their Realtor cousin to show it to them. In any case, that accommodating floor person's opportunity call will have gone with the wind.

There is one exception to the rule. When an ad call comes in about a rental unit in an apartment building, your seasoned agents will not want to spend the time and the gasoline showing it unless the potential gross commission is over $400. If the commission is less than $400, agents should be allowed to give out the address. If the ad caller likes the looks of the building, she can make an appointment with the floor person to inspect the unit. If she gets her brother-in-law to write up a deposit receipt, no big deal.

7

Mini-Bonding

A clever floor person answers the ad caller's first question or two, then cleverly guides the caller into talking about her housing needs, attitudes about real estate, family situation, and pastimes. The floor person will need to keep the caller in conversation long enough to establish his own credibility as a nonpushy professional and to initiate a sort of mini-bonding with the aim of meeting his own objectives.

Mini-bonding establishes rapport in conversation. While the ad caller's objective in conversation is to gain information, the floor person's objective is to gain a personal client. After the floor person has presented the information initially requested, she must next work to present herself as the sort of professional with whom it would be a pleasure to work.

Sell Yourself

Someone, long ago, advised salespeople: "First sell yourself." Realty salespeople tend to overwork that advice. Frequently realty agents spend so much time selling themselves to ad callers that the subject of real estate hardly comes up in conversation. Some such chatty Cathies come across on the telephone as housewives with time on their hands or self-important so-and-sos.

All realty offices have compulsive self-sellers on their staffs. They have grandmothers who consider having "adorable" grandchildren to be their greatest accomplishment in life and proceed to tell everyone about them, including ad callers.

Birds-of-a-feather like to work together. If the caller identifies herself as a grandmother, cool. That floor lady can mini-bond, while sticking to real estate, by telling the ad caller that her grandchildren would dearly love Grandma to own a condo with a swimming pool. That's enough self-selling to establish rapport. Let the caller do the prattling about grandkids.

Does your office have a la-de-da Lucy who has to tell callers about her membership in the country club and her night at the opera ball? Saying "Would you care to have lunch at my club one day?" is enough to establish Lucy's social standing.

Realty offices usually have an expert Elsie, or two, who can and does pontificate on every subject from loan packages to the correct method of decanting fine wine. Just "I have information on those subjects" would be sufficient to let callers know that Elsie is well informed.

Most realty offices have their in-house longevity Len, who bores on and on with every ad caller about his long years in the business, his long marriage, and his long membership in Rotary. (Good grief, when is he ever going to ask for the order?) Callers often prefer working with an experienced agent. By simply saying "I've been selling homes here in Cripple Creek pret' near twenty years now," Len could quickly let his caller know that he is a seasoned agent.

Introduce your credentials. Don't belabor them. Brief self-selling does wonders for establishing rapport. It starts the ball of communication rolling. But forget the autobiography. Be brief or "Just stick to the facts, ma'am."

Be a Good Listener

To gather mini-bonding and self-selling clues, be a good listener. A good listener on the telephone is not a silent listener, however. If an ad caller hears nothing, as she prattles on, she will think she has been cut off or she will think she is speaking to a disinterested party. The caller needs to know that she has a live one on the other end of the line. So the floor person should be prepared to interject now and then, just to let the caller know that he is still with her:

1. "Oh!"
2. "You don't say?"

7

3. "Come again."
4. "Ha ha!"
5. "How smart!"
6. "How clever!"
7. "How funny!"
8. "Yep."
9. "Mmm?"
10. "Uh huh."

Mix up your interjections during the course of the caller's dialogue. Don't belabor just one. (Uncle Bill used to mutter the same "uh huh" at regular intervals when we nieces and nephews told him our stories. We could tell by his repeated "uh huhs" that he was half asleep. No matter, the other uncles would not sit still at all for our chatter. In those days, children were to be seen and not heard.)

By Thy Voice Alone I Should Know Thee?

How is one to figure out the character of an ad caller in order to best tailor conversation? Wouldn't it be nifty if we all had video phones so that we could have a good look at the people who call in on our ads? We could check out their clothing. We could check out their facial expressions. We could check out their body language. Alas, realty agents do not have video phones yet. If we ever do get them, I doubt that ad callers will click themselves up on some strange Realtor's screen.

The ad that draws the call tells a lot about the caller. Singles call about studio condos. Parents call on ads that praise the local school. Sportsmen ask about RV parking. Investors call on ads that mention the current rental value.

Sometimes our immediate assumptions are incorrect, however. I received an ad call on a very large house from a very young couple. I took the couple to see that house. I took them to see another that was closer to schools, in an area better known as a family neighborhood. I assumed that the couple intended to fill a large house with babies. The young couple obviously liked the second house a lot. But when the owner counted out the dozens of little ones on the block, my young couple made a hasty retreat. I never heard from them again. Later I found out that this couple, with movie contacts, led a very glamorous life. They had no intention of having their lifestyle inhibited by youngsters. I had made an assumption that cost me a commission.

Mind your assumptions. Don't jump too fast to conclusions. Wealthy people could be looking to buy an inexpensive starter home for their newlywed offspring. Some vigorous seniors don't mind stairs. They might be hankering for Nautilus equipment, in fact. Would you believe, a childless couple bought an eight-bedroom mansion across from the Hillsborough Elementary School just to house inherited furniture?

Who Is the Phantom Caller?

It is difficult for an agent to guide productive conversation with only an ad to go on. Is she speaking to a hausfrau or a fashion model? Is she speaking to an executive or a hard hat?

Keeping the profiles of typical ad callers in mind can help one to get a fix on the phantom caller. Ad callers fall into two major categories: "haftas" and "phony-phoners."

The haftas are the callers we all pray for. They are the ones who have to buy or sell a property in the foreseeable future.

The phony-phoners are those callers who have no intention of ever buying or selling a house, at least not with the company they are calling. Phony-phoners drive floor persons up the walls. But we are not going to be driven up the walls, are we? We know that anyone with whom we come in contact is a potential for good referrals and/or good free public relations for us.

The Haftas

1. In-Bound Transferees
2. Out-Bound Transferees
3. Recent Sellers
4. 1031 Investors
5. Expanding Families
6. Newlyweds
7. Newly Divorced
8. New Tycoons
9. Empty Nesters
10. Hard Timers

1. The best **in-bound transferees** are those who have just arrived in town. Dad, Mom, and the three kids are in a motel. The dog's in a kennel. The furniture is en route in the van. Second best is the transferee who is already working at the new job while the wifey is stuck back home worried to death about all the cute young things in her husband's new office.

2. Out-bound transferees hafta sell their present homes in order to buy another in their new places of business.

3. Recent sellers have sold their existing home before finding another. They may be dissatisfied with the home-searching activities of their listing agent. Or they might be getting just plain antsy, so they are searching on their own.

4. 1031 investors are those who have sold investment properties and must purchase "like property" within a short time frame in order to avoid paying capital gains taxes.

5. There are **expanding families**, expecting twins we hope, who hafta get out of one-bedroom condos.

6. Newlyweds, these days, look to home ownership. Some two-career newlyweds have saved cash for a down payment, others have indulgent parents. (Don't count on commissions from the ones who have read *No Money Down*.)

7. The **newly divorced**, or those going through the process, will be selling their existing homes and splitting up the proceeds. One or the other may want you to find a new home in which to invest half the proceeds. An agent who is very, very clever (and a real glutton for punishment) might represent both in selling the existing home, and even represent each in his/her home finding searches.

8. Some **new tycoons**, who have struck it rich, will have been advised by their accountants to access the tax deferment of home mortgage interest payments.

9. **Empty nesters** don't stay in the dear old family home forever anymore. They buy down to easy-maintenance no-hassle housing, encouraged by the over fifty-five, $125,000 tax exemption, and by all the senior citizen travel delights they read about in AARP's *Modern Maturity*.

10. **Hard timers** are those poor guys who have lost their jobs, failed in the stock market, or suffered a big lawsuit. They have to sell their homes in order to free up equity for living expenses. They, most of all, need the help of well-trained, empathetic, service-minded professionals.

The Phony-Phoners
1. Nosy Neighbors
2. Personal Estate-Planners

7

3. **Naughty Realty Agents**
4. **New Licensees**
5. **Equal Housing Advocates**
6. **Attackers**
7. **Lonely Folks**
8. **FSBOs**
9. **No-Show SOBs**
10. **Heavy Breathers**

1. A lot of **nosy neighbors** who call in have seen a for-sale sign go up. Others have spied on Realtor types entering their neighbor's home. Some nosy neighbors have read the Sunday open ads or have guessed that a blind ad was written on a neighbor's home. They want to know the asking price, the reason for their neighbor's move, where he's going, if the sellers are splitting up.

2. Personal estate-planners may be looking up ads on properties that are comparable to their own properties. They are in the process of calculating their net worth. They call real estate offices for a free evaluation of their homes. "Just give me a ballpark over the phone," they say. Like all ad callers, estate-planners are a potential for future business. The floor person should advise the caller that she cannot be held accountable for "over the phone, ballpark" evaluations. Instead, "I will come right over to your home and give you a proper evaluation, free of charge." That's called an "appointment"!

3. Naughty realty agents who don't identify themselves are probably doing-the-paper.

4. New licensees who don't identify themselves are probably checking out offices to see which ones sound the best before they call for interviews.

5. There are **equal housing advocates** who call realty offices, usually at random, to check for evidence of discrimination.

6. **Attackers** are cranks looking for a place to vent their anger. In reality, the floor person is not the target, it just feels that way.

One December our floor person got lambasted by an "attacker" for a Christmas card sent out by one of our agents as a prospecting tool. "What does this stupid picture of a crazy dressed up like Mrs. Santa Claus mean, anyway?" The floor person did not defend. She might have explained, "Ma'am, this was a community service project. Our agent, 'Mrs. Claus,' visits schools in her horse and buggy every holiday season." Instead, the floor person merely thanked the cranky woman for her comments and promised that her name would be deleted from the agent's database. *(Qui s'excuse s'accuse.)* The troops decided that the crank was smarting over a "whopping big" real estate commission or that her roof was leaking. We canceled the classified ad referring to our civic minded Mrs. Santa Claus.

7. **Lonely folks** like to talk with nice Realtors. Real estate people are interesting people to talk to. It's said that Realtors know more about their community than the town council does.

Lonely folks can be a nuisance to floor persons who are pressed to do-the-paper, and who do not wish to be distracted should a golden hafta call come in. Be kind, floor person. You'll get your reward in heaven, if not in the wallet.

8. Sharp **FSBOs** call to check out comparables they've spotted in the paper in order to price their own properties. They call to learn telephone techniques from the professionals.

9. SOBs make appointments with floor persons and don't turn up.

10. Heavy breathers, luckily, don't call realty offices often. On one of the unlucky days, the floor person came running into my office. She slammed the door behind her, a sure sign of trouble. "Oh Mrs. T., Mrs. T., I thought it was an ad call. The man wants me to come over to his house and take photos of his privates by candlelight!" "I am so sorry, dear," I said, "but don't we all look prettier by candlelight?" Humor helps in crisis situations.

Phony-phoners, who almost never give their right names, are an annoyance. Realty agents should hang in there with them anyway. I am convinced that phony-phoners eventually direct business to real estate offices, providing that floor persons handle their calls with courtesy.

FSBOs are very apt to come back with business after they have become disenchanted playing the real estate game. Nosy neighbors may talk up listings around town, no charge. Even attackers might end up eating out of the floor person's hand just because the floor person was the only person they yelled at that day who didn't yell back.

I Beg Your Pardon, Sir...

Haftas and phony-phoners alike can be quite rude to a floor person, until he has them eating out of his hand. It seems like realty agents are not the best-loved people in the whole world. No doubt it is the "whopping big" commissions we make. Philippe Plouvier, a French financier, once told me, "It is *internationale, ma chérie.* People do not like to pay commission."

Don't beat yourself up if you should get provoked and lose it. We Realtors are human too.

I received an up call from a woman who identified herself as a hafta. After having answered her laundry list of questions, I asked for her name. "Oh, I'm not telling you my name. I don't want to be bothered by brokers," she said. I let fly. "Well, I bothered to speak with you for fifteen minutes. I told you *my* name." I wonder how much ill will I created for myself with that outburst?

Skip the Techno Terms

Warn your class not to use technical terms of the trade when speaking to ad callers. An ad caller will not continue the conversation if he is made to feel stupid because he does not understand real estate jargon. Here are some are examples of terms best avoided when talking with "civilians":

1. Cash Down
2. Buy-down
3. 72 Hour Kick-out
4. Escrow
5. Prelim
6. Topo
7. Regulation Z
8. Fannie Mae
9. Ginnie Mae
10. Bridge Loan
11. Wrap-around
12. Parol
13. Mansard
14. Hip Roof
15. FSBO
16. Pocket Listing
17. MLS
18. NAR
19. CC&R's
20. PITI

7

Don't correct your ad caller's own peculiar brand of "techno terms." If your caller asks you about a "deal," don't say "transaction, sir." If he calls you a "Real-a-tor," grin and bear it. If she calls Coldwell Banker "Banker Coldwell," tee-hee, she won't be able to find that competitor in the white pages.

More Semantics

Industrial and business psychologists and human rights advocates have had a rum-go at semantics. Supposedly, some jobs were made more dignified when titles were changed. Janitors are now known as "custodians." Laundry men are known as "textile maintenance engineers." Secretaries are "administrative assistants." Sales agents are "representatives." We don't work, we "facilitate." We aren't hired, we are "engaged" or we become "affiliated."

Before equal rights for women was an issue, masculine gender was accepted in representing both males and females, for example: "chairman," "floorman," "salesman," and in contracts: "He shall abide by the provisions..." These days we are supposed to neutralize gender, or give equal coverage to both sexes, particularly when addressing the public: "chairperson," "floor person," "sales representatives," "He/She/They shall abide by the provisions..." Had I written *From Ads to Riches* twenty-five years ago, you would not find nearly so many "shes" in the text. (My politically correct grandchildren call their politically correct grandmother "Grandmother Sir.")

The National Association of Realtors advises its members not to use the word appraisal, unless one has credentials. So we Realtors "evaluate" property instead.

Sales "representatives" are told by psychologists that the verbs "sell," "selling," "buy," and "purchase" are perceived as words of aggression when used by a salesperson. In your telephone techniques training talk about "sell," "selling," "buy," and "purchase." If a floor person, by avoiding those four words at the onset of conversation, is able to put ad callers at ease, it's worth the effort.

Forbid your receptionist to say "sales" agent when she redirects ad calls.

Unfortunately, our advisors have not yet found a suitable substitute for the dirty "C" word, "commission."

There is less liability in the spoken word than in the written word. Still it would be a good idea to review attorney Hugh Connolly's warning on pages 73–74, during your telephone training session.

Be Positive Even If It Hurts

The American public shops when it is happy. So, by all means, your public should be kept happy. Keep the "negs" out of your telephone conversation. The more cheerful the conversation, the more favorably the caller will think of playing real estate with the salesperson with whom he is speaking.

One mustn't think one can threaten a prospective buyer into action. No home is the last one in the world. Are interest rates really going to spike next week? You are not the only ethical agent in town.

A floor person must not be lured, by a caller, into a can-you-top-this discussion of the misdeeds of competitors. That kind of talk boomerangs. One mustn't have-at-it at the expense of the lending industry. Most prospective buyers will have no choice but to deal with a professional lender eventually. One can discuss the trauma of renovation, as opposed to buying a new home, but one must not dramatize it.

During the worst of recessions, one must not talk doom and gloom (sometimes a mediocre agent's excuse for his own lack of production). Floor persons should always sound jolly like the Anns.

Don't Be a Clown

Be jolly like the Anns, but be careful. Using humor in ad copy is a way of telling readers that real estate is fun, and that they need not be afraid of "hard sell" when they make contact with a realty office.

The ad writer is protected by her proofreaders. Telling funny stories to strangers on the telephone, however, without a proofreader's protection is risky business. The floor person's brand of humor, his grin unseen, could be misunderstood. What would an American caller think if she heard Roy Brooks's style of humor over the blower? Sounding jolly is fun enough.

Shh...Use Discretion...

Trainees must be reminded, "For mercy sakes, be discreet." "Don't let expert Elsies who know all tell all." Indiscretions could get back to sellers, thereby putting the company listings in jeopardy. Don't tell about a client's divorce. Don't reveal that a client lost his job. Don't report on a customer's family tree. Don't be an erring expert Elsie who says something like: "My client has just been promoted to president of Greenhouse Limited. I'm one of the very first to know."

The author was listing agent for Patty Hearst's family home at the time of her kidnapping. The property was advertised frequently in classified. Never was the name of the owners revealed. While a public relations opportunity was ignored, a display of indiscretion could have done permanent damage to our business. "Glass, china, and reputation are easily crack'd and never well mended." So said newspaperman Benjamin Franklin.

Curious ad callers adore hearing the inside scoop about real estate clients, particularly the rich and famous. Those same curious callers will be afraid to work with any real estate agent who demonstrates that he is willing to talk about clients' personal affairs.

Don't Rush It

Reaching a state of excellence in floor duty telephone techniques is not as easy as it was talking on a toy phone. Suggest to your trainees that they schedule some in-the-shower think time and some in-front-of-the-mirror rehearsal time to perfect telephone techniques.

When that up desk ring-a-ding-dings, floor persons ought be prepared to spend as much as fifteen minutes with a first-time caller. It takes a pack of good listening, some manipulation, a lot of biting-the-lip to score. But, heck, ad call conversation takes less time, and a lot less money, than treating prospects to lunch.

Keep It Rollin', Rollin', Rollin'

With due diligence on the part of the manager, lessons taught will be established as habit within three weeks. To maintain the habit and enthusiasm for classified, it would be wise to make classified a regular part of sales meetings. Report on transactions generated by ad calls. Encourage agents to tell about successful or amusing ad calls. Applaud those who have scored.

Enjoy the Game

Hey, champeens, the floor game is great sport. "Firm grip, now." "Nice serve!" "Good rally!" "Your point, Mr. Floorman!"

To Agents

I hope you're not irked by my caricatures of real estate types. I'm one of you, you know. Some of my old teammates can tell you that there was a time when I was your typical prima donna sales agent. I carry an ancient Vuitton wallet. And I sure have bungled my share of ad calls.

The FSBO Follies

8

For sale by owner… You have decided not to list your property with a professional. You are going to market it all by yourself.

Congratulations on your bravery! This is a big job to take on. Real estate is probably the most valuable commodity you will sell in your lifetime. Nevertheless, you are confident that you are a property owner who is equipped to do so. You are experienced in real estate transactions. You are comfortable with contracts and other documents. You have good negotiation techniques… Besides, you were not pleased with your last realty agent. And most important, you do not want to pay any more "whopping big" real estate commissions!

Congratulations for taking the time to research the marketing process. By reading this book, written for real estate professionals, you have joined the ranks of the real estate wise. You probably will be one of the few FSBOs who end up selling their property by themselves without getting a real estate agent involved. That is, if you hit advertising hard and heavy.

8

Heavy advertising is crucial to the sale of any property that is not being marketed through the real estate industry.

FSBOs do not have access to the professionals' built-in customer base, referral systems, computer network, and conditioned public awareness. FSBOs do not have fat prospect books. FSBOs do not have skilled associates to help them sell. Not having all those professional facilitators, FSBOs are obliged to market their product directly to the public.

It is impossible, however, to accurately target the public sector in which your potential buyers may be found. Demographic studies will fool you. Therefore, FSBOs are advised to cover all bases by advertising their product for sale to a population of thousands, in a variety of locations. (Word-of-mouth and yard signs alone won't cut it. This is a numbers game.) Because of its affordability, as well as its broad coverage, classified advertising is, obviously, the only way to go.

Before you commence your for-sale-by-owner advertising campaign, there are certain preparations that you must make:

1. **Set the Price**
2. **Sparkle Up the Property**
3. **Collect Documents**
4. **Get a Real Estate Attorney**
5. **Get a Yard Sign**
6. **Prepare Fact Sheets**
7. **Set a Time Limit**
8. **Set Up Phone Systems**
9. **Have a Family Pow-Wow**
10. **Buy a Rabbit's Foot**

1. Set the price *right.* Don't try on any old price for size. If you overprice, you won't sell. If you underprice, you will sell, then punish yourself forever.

Take heed. The price you ask is not to be determined by the price you want. The correct price you ask is close to the price that a qualified buyer is willing to pay. That correct asking price is based on what similar properties have sold for within the past twelve months, or within the past six months in a lively market, and on what is being asked for similar properties currently for sale on the open market. Add up the prices of those similar properties, after throwing out the most expensive and the least expensive. Then divide the sum of the remainder by the number of the properties. The figure you get will be a suitable asking price (providing your property isn't a pigsty, providing it doesn't have a valuable extra like a tennis court or a celebrity neighbor. In such cases you will make adjustments). If you're looking for a fast sale, don't price your property one penny higher than your closest competition, no matter how special the extras in yours.

Caution: People who sell by themselves are perceived to be somewhat greedy. Don't affirm that perception with a "greedy" price. You'll drive off customers.

You can get price information about similar properties, "comparables," by asking around. Mind you, neighbors, even buyers and sellers, don't always tell a true story.

You can get accurate information from escrow or title officers, for sure, if you tell them that you will place your escrow with them when the property sells. They can give you a computer printout of the completed sales of the "comps" in your area.

You might get the information by playing "phony-phoner." Tell the nice floor person in a local realty office that you are thinking of listing your property with her company and could she, please, make up a "comp" list for you.

You can get information by reading classified every day for a couple of weeks. The open house section of the Sunday newspaper will steer you to comparables for sale so that you can go make your own on-site evaluations on weekends.

2. Sparkle up your property. Paint, scrub, straighten closets, eliminate clutter, weed, prune, rototill the back forty. Fuss-budget neat gives potential buyers confidence. Buy flowers. Borrow lamps.

8

Load up on air freshener. Ask your interior decorator friend to give your place the once-over. Pretend you're hosting a wedding reception.

3. **Collect** examples of all the **documents** you will be using in the process of selling your property. Study them. Should the God of FSBOs send you a qualified buyer quick, you will want to be well prepared in advance for negotiations.

You will need deposit receipts/purchase agreement forms. Be sure the forms are currently in use in your area. The date of printing should appear somewhere on the first page. Chances are that the forms you signed when you last purchased real estate have been considerably updated.

Since it is very unlikely that you will accept any offer in its entirety, get some counteroffer forms. You don't want to be scribbling changes on the deposit receipt. Some legal types won't accept inserts and cross-outs on contracts.

Get yourself some structural disclosure forms. Most states require that sellers present buyers with a comprehensive disclosure statement that is meant primarily to reveal all defects, such as drainage problems, leaks, toxins, and noise pollution. While you fill in the blanks you will get a fix on what corrections ought to be made before you expose your property to the public.

You can buy forms at the local stationer's. Be sure that they are no more than two years old. Maybe a title/escrow company can provide you with what you need. Maybe your local board of Realtors will share. Probably, you can find a nice realty agent who will give you a complete packet of all documents pertaining to the sale of residential property. Or ask a Realtor for the name and phone number of one of those commercial companies that sell standard real estate forms in your state.

Collect some rate sheets from institutional lenders. Usually offers to purchase are made contingent upon the buyer securing a loan at a specified interest rate. Before you agree to accept an offer with a loan contingency, you'll want to know that the interest rate and loan fees identified in the deposit receipt are logical.

NCR (No Carbon Required)

COUNTER OFFER

Date: _____ Time: _____

In response to the OFFER ☐ TO PURCHASE, ☐ TO EXCHANGE, ☐ TO LEASE — ☐ the real property, ☐ the business, ☐ the premises — commonly known as: _____

_____, herein referred to as Offeror,

made by _____

_____, the following counter offer is hereby submitted:

U. S. Department of Housing and Urban Development

NOTICE TO PURCHASERS OF HOUSING CONSTRUCTED BEFORE 1978

WATCH OUT FOR LEAD-BASED PAINT POISONING!

If the home you intend to purchase was built before 1978, it may contain lea...
out of every four pre-1978 buildings have lead-based paint.

YOU NEED TO P...

NCR (No Carbon Required)

AGREEMENT TO OCCUPY PRIOR TO CLOSE OF ESCROW

_____, Purchaser, having heretofore executed an Agreement of Sale dated _____ 19____,
in the City of _____, County of _____, State of _____

_____ to obtaining title thereto, the parties agree as follows:

_____ permission to Purchaser to take

NCR (No Carbon Required)

REAL ESTATE TRANSFER DISCLOSURE STATEMENT
(STATUTORY FORM)

THIS DISCLOSURE STATEMENT CONCERNS THE REAL PROPERTY SITUATED IN THE CITY OF _____, COUNTY OF _____, STATE OF CALIFORNIA, DESC...

THIS STATEMENT IS A DISCLOSURE OF THE CONDITION OF THE ABOVE DESCRIBED PRO...
WITH SECTION 1102 OF THE CIVIL CODE AS OF _____, 19___
ANY KIND BY THE SELLER(S) OR ANY AGENT(S) REPRESENTING ANY PRIN...
IS NOT A SUBSTITUTE FOR ANY INSPECTIONS OR WARRANTIES THE...

1. COORDINATION WITH OTHER DISCLOSURE FORMS

This Real Estate Transfer Disclosure Statement is made pursuant to S...
the details of the particular real estate transaction (for exam...
Substituted Disclosures: The following disclosu...
disclosure obligations on this form, whe...

HAZARDOUS MATERIALS DISCLOSURE

...GREEMENT, ☐ EXCHANGE AGREEMENT, ☐ LEASE AGREEMENT covering the real

...perty may contain materials that have
...may need to be specially han-
...other electrical compo-
...as fire-proof-
...n cur-

EQUAL HOUSING OPPORTUNITY

REAL ESTATE PURCHASE CONTRACT AND RECEIPT FOR DEPOSIT

REGIONAL DATA SERVICE

This is more than a receipt for money. This is intended to be a legally binding contract. Read it carefully.

RECEIVED FROM_____
sum set forth in Paragraph 1.A below as a deposit on account of the purchase price of _____
$ _____, California _____
_____ for the purchase of property situated in _____
_____, State of California, described _____

upon the following terms and conditions:
1. FINANCING TERMS:
   A. DEPOSIT evidenced by ☐ person...
   deposited in ☐ Esc..., which ...
   B. ADDITION...
   in th...

...FOREIGN SELLER AFFIDAVIT

...Computer Alignment

8

4. **Get a real estate attorney.** No matter how many properties you have sold successfully in the past, no matter how confident you are in your knowledge of real estate, please, protect yourself by having a real estate attorney approve all documents you sign. A corporate or a tax attorney will not do. You need a real estate specialist who is involved daily in the complex business of transferring property in accordance with the variables of law and local standards of practice.

In some states you have no choice. By law, you must employ an attorney, because attorneys do the title search and prepare escrow papers. Whether an attorney is mandated in your state or not you can get names of local real estate attorneys from your board of Realtors, from the bar association, or in the yellow pages of the telephone directory.

You will need to alert the attorney of your choice that you will be requiring his services before your buyer appears on the scene. Tell the attorney that you will be wanting him to approve the purchase agreement that you will be signing. If you are squeamish about working with documents, you might ask him to fill out the entire purchase agreement for you and your buyer. You want him to be willing to use standard forms because if he draws up an agreement from scratch, you will be paying a hefty fee for his "billable hours." Besides, the standard forms used by realty professionals in your area are familiar documents. They will be easier for your buyer and his lender to understand than an attorney's original "legalese."

5. **Get a yard sign.** Before you do, check with your city hall to be sure you are permitted to have a sign. If you are permitted to have one, find out about the size and color restrictions. You may have to buy a permit. If you are selling a unit in a complex, check sign regulations with the homeowners association. You don't want to spend money on a sign you can't use.

Find out where you are allowed to install your sign. Police departments and homeowners associations often impose fines for misplaced signs.

Have a professional sign maker make your sign. The red-and-white jobs sold in hardware stores will do nothing to enhance the image of your property.

Be sure that your phone number is painted on bold enough to be read from the street. Be sure to include "By Appointment Only."

Whether or not "For Sale by Owner" is printed on your sign is up to you, unless the local ordinance requires such identification. There are good reasons for on and good reasons for off. Buyers who, like you, prefer to go it alone will like to know that they will be dealing directly with the owner. So will those who fancy themselves to be hot-shot negotiators. Timid souls and those who have had good experiences working with real estate professionals may be reluctant to telephone for an appointment when they see on the sign that it's the owner himself with whom they must deal.

Caution: Be prepared for buyers who expect to share in the commission dollars you save.

6. **Prepare fact sheets** to pass out to prospects who inspect the property. Note the address, your phone number, and your name. List the rooms: bedrooms, bathrooms, dining room, and so on. Add the amenities: the swimming pool, storage facilities, proximity to public transportation and schools. If your roof or furnace is less than two years old, put that down. Don't forget the asking price.

7. **Set your time limit.** Establish the exact length of time that you will spend marketing your property by yourself before you turn the job over to the professionals.

Real estate that remains on the market too long becomes stale. The longer it remains unsold, the more the public respect for the property dwindles and so does the eventual sales price. Buyers are wont to say, "How long has it been on the market?" and "Why hasn't it sold yet?"

For a residence, three months for-sale-by-owner is generally maximum. Since vacant land takes longer to sell, a year may not be too long for a FSBO to hang in there.

8

Do not extend your set termination date by so much as one day, even if a guy has been back to see the property four times or if he says he plans to make an offer when he returns from vacation. List with a professional anyway. You can persuade a listing agent to exclude that particular guy from your agreement to pay commission, or full commission, should the guy actually turn up with an acceptable offer after you have signed the listing agreement.

8. **Set up efficient phone systems** that guard against losing prospects. Ad callers tend to be impatient. If they don't receive prompt attention, they may have some realty friend follow up for them. More often, they just lose interest.

If there is no articulate adult on the premises twenty-four hours a day, you will need to install a mechanical device to take calls in your absence.

You can equip your telephone with an answering machine that records incoming calls. It should be programmed to respond with something like "Thank you for calling 123-5555," or "Thank you for calling about the home for sale. Please leave your name and telephone number. We will return your call within two hours." You will be able to do so because the machine you purchase will have a function that makes it possible for you to check your messages from an outside phone.

The call-forwarding function, which your telephone company can provide for you, would allow you to redirect incoming calls to wherever you may be: your place of business, your sweety's apartment. Be certain that only you, or a knowledgeable assignee, picks up the redirected phone calls.

If you have a bunch of phone freaks in your household, you would be wise to have your phone company install a temporary separate sacred phone in your home, with a number different from that of the family phone, to use in your advertising and on your sign. Equip it with its own answering machine or call-forwarding function. Keep it sacred. No outgoing calls allowed.

9. **Call a family pow-wow.** Explain your marketing strategy and what to expect. Emphasize the importance of family cooperation. Establish the rules:

A. Only adults may answer incoming calls.

B. Only adults may show the property.

C. No one shall be admitted to the property without an appointment.

D. The property will not be shown at night to strangers unless there are two or more adults in attendance. The same applies to properties located in remote areas and to unoccupied properties, day or night. (When residential real estate is advertised in the newspaper, on a sign, over the radio, wherever, it is illegal to deny an opportunity to inspect that real estate to anyone. So, if you feel nervous about showing to a stranger, arrange for a first meeting in a "safety zone": at your office, in your bank, or at the public library.)

E. Everyone should avoid lengthy conversations with prospects, to safeguard against future "he said, she said" confrontations. No one should answer questions about the neighborhood or the condition of the property. Let the fact sheets do the talking.

F. Courtesy is an absolute requirement, even when speaking with pesky realty agents who call on FSBO ads. They certainly will call unless there is a glut of good properties on the market. "Principals Only" in ads will not keep them away. As a FSBO, you might need a realty agent one day (85 percent of FSBOs end up selling their properties with the help of a real estate professional). You don't want it said, in the marketplace, that the owner is a scrooge.

Granted, almost all realty agents who call on FSBO ads are looking for listings. Some are honest about that. Some others, not so honest, will say that they have a serious prospect for the property when they do not. Some agent callers may actually have serious prospects. Let them show the property. Encourage them to write up offers. (Take it from a realty veteran, you should look positively at a bird in hand. Be willing to pay a real estate agent his selling commission for a transaction that meets your requirements. You will get your money's worth because that selling agent will automatically handle many of the tasks, free of charge, that you would be paying a listing agent to handle.)

G. All occupants are expected to keep their personal spaces squeaky clean and prissy neat. All occupants are expected to help KP the rest of the premises before showings. That means to pick up the toys, air out the kitchen, hide the kitty's litter box, etc.

It may take more than a family pow-wow to assure cooperation if you have teenage boys in the house. They tend to be grumpy when their home is being shown. They tend to leave "dead" sweat socks and moldy ice cream cartons around their bedrooms. I knew one young man who lit up a joint every time prospects entered the house. You may have to offer your teenage son a bribe. (If you are a landlord selling an occupied rental, you may want to offer your tenants a bribe to ensure cooperation.)

10. Buy yourself a rabbit's foot. Everyone who has real estate for sale, FSBOs and pros alike, good times and bad, could use some luck to go along with the most dynamite classified advertising…

"The Time Has Come, the Walrus Said"

To write of many things… Once you've done all your prepping, like a good house painter, the time has come for "Ready, Get Set, Write." Turn on your Tensor light. Review chapters 3 and 4 of *From Ads to Riches*. Then write yourself a totally awesome ad. Type it up nice and neat, double or triple space it. Add your name, phone number, and address.

Take your first ad to the newspaper office. The next ones you can fax in. Become buddies with the classified personnel. They can help you fine-tune your copy. They will help you place your ad in the most appropriate section of classified. They can tell you which days pull the most. They will quote deadlines, and explain the cost structure and billing procedures.

You will want to ask the buddies who is to be your contact at the newspaper. You will want to ask how to make last-minute deletions or changes once the copy is at the paper. You will want to decide how often you will advertise. Unless the buddies have advice to the contrary, you should advertise at least four times a week to reach the required multitudes. (Statisticians have drawn up impressive charts, tables, and formulas to show market penetration results from various types of media promotion. These analogies are always skewed by local conditions: market climate, economics, local newspaper circulation, weather, and the copywriter's skill. So, just cover your bases with the four-times-a-week formula.)

You will ask the buddies to help you get the most mileage out of your advertising budget. Maybe, for only a few dollars more, you could advertise six times a week instead of four and/or have your ads repeated in satellite newspapers. Maybe the buddies would give you a discount for signing up for a certain number of lines per month. Maybe you are eligible for a discount on your personal property ads if your company is a big contract advertiser. Maybe the newspaper has some freebies.

Finally, when satisfied that you have done everything that an accomplished full-service classified copywriter needs to do, you may look forward to the wild excitement of seeing your dynamite advertising copy in print for the very first time. Try, accomplished classified copywriter, not to lose that wild excitement. You must not slack off until you have in your possession a signed purchase agreement, approved by your real estate attorney, and a cleared deposit check.

To Agents

You may be wondering why a licensed real estate broker would give advice to those who choose not to hire us.

Well, first of all, those FSBOs have already made up their minds to go it alone. Second, the more they know about the complexities and hard work that goes into selling real estate, the more they are apt to put in with professionals.

Should you attend a Joan Tayler success seminar, you will find "FSBOs as a Source of Listings" prominent on the agenda. Attendees are advised:

> *Call on FSBO ads. Offer to deliver to the owner, free of charge, a packet of the documents she will be needing: Purchase Contract and Receipt for Deposit, Counteroffer forms, Structural Disclosure form, Financial Disclosure form, Affidavit of Non-foreign Status, examples of pest control and structural inspection reports.*
>
> *You will not be so generous as to translate the language contained in those ominous documents for her or to teach her how to use them, will you?"*

According to the NAR *Code of Ethics and Standards of Practice,* Article 9-4:

> *Realtors shall not offer a service described as "free of charge" when the rendering of a service is contingent on the obtaining of a benefit such as a listing or commission.*

This language, pertaining to service, has been interpreted to include intent.

To get back in the door, call the FSBO again. Offer to deliver some additional real estate data. How about articles on asbestos, radon, or landfill and copies of your company's best classified ads?

The FSBO will be grateful for your many gifts. She may feel obligated to list with you when she decides to give up her "second job."

Be My Guest

Every copywriter gets writer's block, sooner or later. Every copywriter gets a bug, gets exhausted, loses the passion. Even if a copywriter has a shoe box full of ideas, a dictionary, a thesaurus, an encyclopedia, a complete set of *One Hundred Great Books,* subscriptions to two newspapers and four magazines, a cassette collection, and the public library right next door, there are times when she could use a handout, a gift of ready-made ads to tide her over until she is back in the saddle again. Be my guest.

Maybe the boss has not hired a copywriter and is doing the writing himself, but not well. Maybe the troops are doing the writing, but not well. This office could use a head start. As Conrad Hilton would say, "Be my guest."

Here are 100 JM Tayler & Company Realtors ads, just as they were printed in the newspapers. All made the phones ring. None got us into trouble. Some pulled well enough to be repeated. Many pulled callers who became our buyers or sellers. They brought us new recruits. Quite a number of these ads were quoted at cocktail parties. Altogether they brought us the jealousy of sales agents in other offices where our kind of advertising was not provided. They are yours to repeat word for word, punctuation by punctuation. They are yours to print in part or whole, to print upside down, to scramble, to use once or a thousand times. Please, be my guest.

To Agents

If you are producing your own ads, there are probably enough printed here to keep you going for a year or two. They could save you weeks of work. Maybe you'll find that some ads need only a price adjustment.

When you've worn out all 100 finished ads, then pick up some headings from chapter 3 (not Mr. Brooks's), crack your dictionary, and fill in the body copy yourselves. Be my guest.

Location

9

Location is the most important criterion in buyers' search for real estate.

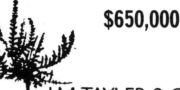

9 Location

9 Architecture

Architecture draws mental pictures.

Architecture

9

9 Special Amenities

Whet appetites with special amenities.

9 Special Amenities

Special Amenities

Children

People with children have more entries in their want lists than most other home buyers.

9 Children

9 Children

Gardening

Gardening is the number-one pastime in the United States.

Gardening

9 Hobbies

People in the United States spend a lot of time on their hobbies.

9 Sports

Americans are sports minded.

9 Holidays

Holidays come along just when tired copywriters need ideas the most.

Weather

Everybody talks about the weather, but no one does anything about it. Do something about it.

Colors

Colors have psychological and esthetic appeal.

9 Colors

Book Titles

Copywriters have home libraries from whence they extract book titles.

CHRISTOPHER ROBIN
SLEPT HERE

Adorable A.A. Milne ENGLISH cottage with POOH BEAR window seat . . . 3 Bedrooms, new kitchen, dining room, darling garden. Close-in westside. Short walk to Agatha's English Tea Room. $229,000.

J M TAYLER & CO.

REALTORS   342-9252
100 EL CAMINO REAL, BURLINGAME

"GONE WITH THE WIND"
COLONIAL

On a level promontory lot in HILLSBOROUGH with a dramatic VIEW of San Francisco and the Bay   Only 5 years old with 4 spacious bedrooms, formal dining room, family room upstairs library, 3 car garage, swimming pool . . . Excellent assumable financing . . . (one of Hillsborough's most beautifully maintained homes) . . . $599,000.

J M TAYLER & CO.

REALTORS   342-9252
100 EL CAMINO REAL, BURLINGAME

9 Song Titles

Popular music titles and lines can be lifted for headlines.

"COUNTRY ROAD TAKE ME HOME"

On Emerald Lakes COUNTRY ROAD. Fixer-upper Country Ranch. 2 Bedrooms, Dining Room. Big Lot. $485,000.

On a quiet Belmont COUNTRY ROAD. Just Listed. Wide open Contempo. 3 Bedrooms, Sausalito Sun Deck. $520,000.

J M TAYLER & CO.
Realtors   342-9252
100 El Camino, Burl.

"STROLLIN' THRU THE PARK.."

"One Day in the Merry Merry Month of May"... Neat-as-a-pin old fashioned SAN MATEO PARK home, short walk to Burlingame Shops... 3 Bedrooms, Formal Dining room, Separate Professional Artist's Studio, Swimming Pool. $425,000.

J M TAYLER & CO.
REALTORS   342-9252
100 EL CAMINO REAL, BURLINGAME

---

9 Money

Money is in every classified reader's mind.

9 Money

Snob Appeal

We all have dreams. Snob appeal ads pull.

9 Snob Appeal

Sex Appeal

Sex appeal is used to sell everything from automobiles to cosmetics to packaged bread.

Even a HOT TUB!

Exciting 3 yr. old Hillsborough home. Much rich natural wood inside and out. Sharp "today" carpets and window coverings. Circular drive, broad deck, smart landscaping. Decorates divinely with contemporary and/or antique furniture. $259,500.

J M TAYLER & CO.

REALTORS   342-9252

100 EL CAMINO REAL, BURLINGAME

FOR LOVERS

Belmont country hideaway. On a tucked-away (but not far away) country road. All warm redwood, with stone paths, oak trees, soft carpets, loft bedroom. UNIQUE . . . SERENE . . . SENSITIVE . . . $103,500.

J M TAYLER & CO.

REALTORS   342-9252

100 EL CAMINO REAL, BURLINGAME

Wrap Up

10

I hope you agree that there are many more uses for classified newsprint than wrapping up the garbage and lining the hamster cage.

Would it be presumptuous to say that what you've learned and taught out of this book will find its way into other areas of your company's activities? Will telephone techniques improve in general? Will the troops' desks become more organized? Will your agents turn out better business letters? Maybe you've picked up a few good ideas for your sales meetings. Have you lowered the stress level on deadline days? Maybe you've had a few chuckles.

Prediction

At year's end, when you review your transaction control sheets, you will see written over and over again something that you may never have seen before:

Source of Client: Classified Ad.

Additional Reading

Ad Aid, Donn May, Marco Island, FL.

Real Estate Advertising, Lawrence J. Danks, Dearborn Financial, Chicago, IL.

Phone Power, George Walther, Berkeley Publishing Group, New York, NY.

How to Say It, Rosalie Maggio, Prentice-Hall, Des Moines, IA.

Lifetime Conversation Guide, James K. Van Fleet, Prentice-Hall, Des Moines, IA.

Unlimited Selling Power, Donald Moine & Kenneth Lloyd, Prentice-Hall, Des Moines, IA.

What America Does Right, Robert H. Waterman, Jr. W.W. Norton, New York, NY.

The following books may be ordered through:

> The California Association of Realtors Supply Center
> 525 South Virgil Avenue
> Los Angeles, CA 90020
> Tel: (213) 739-8227

Simplified Classifieds: 1001 Real Estate Ads That Sell, William H. and Bradley A. Pivar

2,001 Winning Ads for Real Estate, Steve Kennedy and Deborah Johnson

Real Estate Advertising That Works, Linda Lipman

Power Real Estate Advertising, William H. and Bradley A. Pivar

The Real Estate Sales Survival Kit, Doug Malouf and William H. Pivar

Up and Running in Real Estate Sales, P. J. Thompson

Phone Power: Techniques for the Real Estate Professional, Teri and Mike Gamble

Index

About the Author

Former ballet dancer, costume designer, TV director, and Realtor, Joan McLellan Tayler is a well-known character in the field of residential real estate. She has been called "Barracuda," "Tycooness," "A Real Tough Lady," "A Legend," and "A Credit to the Real Estate Industry."

Joan Tayler was born into a pioneer California family during the Great Depression. Her great-grandfather state senator William T. Garratt owned and operated the foundry that made the Golden Spike that linked the Transcontinental Railroad from the East to the West in 1869. Her father, Rod McLellan, a pioneer in the flower business, was known all over the world as the "Orchid King." Her mother, Vivian Goddard, is an esteemed artist, still painting and exhibiting at the age of ninety.

Tayler was raised in the San Francisco Bay Area. She graduated from Sarah Lawrence College in New York, along with the likes of TV star Barbara Walters, author Mary McCarthy, and model Penelope Tree. Her teachers at Sarah Lawrence included philosopher Joseph Campbell, poet Stephen Spender, and sculptor David Smith.

In 1965, Joan Tayler entered the field of real estate on the San Francisco Peninsula, as part-time classified copywriter. She continued writing real estate ad copy for twenty-five years while working as sales agent, office manager, real estate trainer, and finally as founder/owner/administrator of JM Tayler & Company Realtors.

She has served as director on twelve business and civic corporate boards. She is a recognized public speaker. She has published over 15,000 classified newspaper ads!

In 1990, the author sold her beloved JM Tayler & Company Realtors in order to devote more time to family, fly fishing, flowers, fitness, travel, the Arthritis Foundation, and in order to begin yet another career as author of "please pick my brain" real estate books.

Order Form

   If you found this book informative, useful, and enjoyable, why not spread the word to your employees, colleagues, and friends (or use this copy as a workbook and buy another to keep intact)?

   To order copies of *From Ads to Riches,* clip out the form below and mail it with your check or money order, payable to **Mansion Press,** to:

Mansion Press
P.O. Box 2510
Novato, CA 94948
(Fax: 415–883–4280)

- ✂ -

Please send me
   ____copies of *From Ads to Riches* @ $19.95 $_____
   ____copies with professional discount of 10% $_____
      on minimum orders of 10

Shipping and handling (allow 4–6 weeks for delivery)
   first copy, $3.50 $_____
   additional copies, $.50 $_____

California residents please add
   $1.45 per copy toward sales tax $_____
   $1.30 per discounted copy (orders of 10 or more) $_____

TOTAL $_____

Name_____Purchase Order #_____
Company or Organization_____
Address_____
_____
City, State, Zip_____
Phone_____ Fax_____
      (in case we have a question about your order)